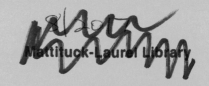

The
NYC
Kitchen
Cookbook

The NYC Kitchen Cookbook

150 RECIPES INSPIRED BY THE
SPECIALTY FOOD SHOPS,
SPICE STORES, AND
MARKETS OF NEW YORK CITY

Tracey Ceurvels

Skyhorse Publishing

Skyhorse Publishing books may be purchased in bulk at special discounts for sales promotion, corporate gifts, fund-raising, or educational purposes. Special editions can also be created to specifications. For details, contact the Special Sales Department, Skyhorse Publishing, 307 West 36th Street, 11th Floor, New York, NY 10018 or info@skyhorsepublishing.com.

Skyhorse® and Skyhorse Publishing® are registered trademarks of Skyhorse Publishing, Inc.®, a Delaware corporation.

Visit our website at www.skyhorsepublishing.com.

10 9 8 7 6 5 4 3 2 1

Library of Congress Cataloging-in-Publication Data is available on file.

Cover design by Jane Sheppard
Cover photography by Tracey Ceurvels, Caroline White, Judy Schiller, Kirsten Kay Thoen, and iStockphoto

Print ISBN: 978-1-5107-2112-8
Ebook ISBN: 978-1-5107-2116-6

Printed in China

This book is dedicated to my wonderful, always loving, and supportive parents, Bill and Yvonne, and to my darling daughter, Sabrina, who, moments ago, told me that one of her favorite activities is baking together.

TABLE OF CONTENTS

INTRODUCTION

There's something special about shopping for food in New York City. Each morning the metal grates of stores rise up, with shop owners ready to sell their herbs, spices, oils, vinegars, wine, cheese, fish, meat, and vegetables. Near our apartments, or only a train ride away, New York City seems to carry every ingredient imaginable—from Chinatown, where vats of fish sit on sidewalks; to the Bronx, where family members of old-world Italian ancestors make crusty bread and handmade pasta; to Brighton Beach where, I've been told, you can buy Russian ingredients no longer available in Russia.

In New York City, you can find mozzarella made moments ago, obscure spices, rare fish, unique cuts of meat, artisanal everything, from honey to beer, and infinite types of handmade pasta in many shapes and colors. You can choose among hundreds of salts, visit a vegetable butcher, find any green under the sun, taste many varieties of olive oil, eat cheese made around the world or from local New York farms, and visit an entire market devoted to Italian food. You may find inspiration in a jar of fenugreek at an Indian store, in cassava at a Brazilian store, tamarind at an Asian market, or berbere, an Ethiopian spice mixture.

Inside these stores, stimulated by scent, color, and flavor, our imaginations flourish

And this seems to be in tandem with the New York experience of picking and choosing from the multitude of offerings, and melting and merging tradition with innovation to create our own enjoyable way of cooking.

There are neighborhoods that still harbor certain types of food, like the stretch of Lexington Avenue in the 20s, which has remained Indian, or the area around Arthur Avenue in the Bronx, which has been Italian since the early 1900s. Other areas have a variety of stores and cuisines. There are two blocks on Bleecker Street where you just might be able to do all your food shopping with a butcher shop, a bread store, a cheese shop, and a pork store. In and around Union Square and Flatiron you could never tire of options to make for dinner.

New York City is truly a food lover's paradise

While I do enjoy dining out frequently (I have many favorite restaurants), and grabbing a snack from one of many food trucks or eating a slice of pizza now and then, what I love most is cooking at home with the ingredients I seek and find during my jaunts around the city.

For one, it helps feed my love of adventure. Visiting different parts of the city and discovering the variety of food and ingredients satiates my sense of wanderlust. Secondly, I enjoy meeting people who love what they do, especially when it comes to food. I've met beer brewers, winemakers, chocolatiers, butchers, and cheese mongers. Their passion for what they do is contagious, and honestly, I'd rather buy an artisanal product made with love and care than a mass-produced one at the supermarket—that's my philosophy.

When I first moved to New York City, I lived in Chinatown, where I became immediately fascinated with the food shops on nearly every block. I started buying ingredients like lemongrass, Thai chili paste, Chinese five-spice, and miso from Asian specialty stores and incorporating them into my daily meals. I'd also walk to nearby Little Italy where Di Palo's became my go-to store for fresh pasta, prosciutto, and Parmesan, and further uptown to the Union Square Greenmarket for fresh and locally-farmed eggs, garlic, and fruits and vegetables.

I ventured to other food stores that inspired me, like Kalustyan's on Lexington Avenue, where I'd stock up on Indian spices and curries. I came to like olives in a roundabout way: I tasted tapenade, that salty delicious spread so sublime on a piece of sliced baguette, and soon found myself at Titan Foods in Astoria, choosing among the vats of olives for dips and recipes (plus feta cheese and phyllo dough). I'd trek to Sahadi's on Atlantic Avenue in Brooklyn Heights for pistachios, spices, and ingredients like rose and orange blossom water and fig glaze. The West Village is home to one of my new favorite stores, The Meadow, which has an entire wall of artisanal chocolate, plus hundreds of unique salts that add new dimensions to food. When I want a mouthwatering cheese, I go to Murray's Cheese, and also Stinky Bklyn, Bedford Cheese, Artisanal, and Saxelby Cheesemongers. For meat, there's Ottomanelli's, Staubitz Market, Esposito & Sons, Fleisher's Grass-Fed & Organic Meats, and one of my favorites: Florence Meat Market. It's tucked away on a charming West Village street, and you can call ahead to owner/butcher Benny to order special cuts of meat.

Oh, and coffee . . . I wasn't a loyal fan until I had a young baby and needed an extra buzz to keep me awake. Fortunately, Roasting Plant was in walking distance. The scent of their coffee beans roasting and then shooting through a tube overhead is something I look forward to every time I go for my stash. The Block Party Blend is my favorite for its notes of chocolate and caramel, and perks me up in the morning as I start my day. I add coffee to several of my recipes, both sweet and savory. Now searching for coffee has become an adventure: Stumptown, Porto Rico Importing, Blue Bottle, and D'Amico are also regular spots to pick up beans.

I can't mention coffee without mentioning tea. I roast chicken with tea leaves and add tea to desserts, and even vegetables. Tea can add both sweet and early nuances to a dish. There are so many tea shops, from Harney & Sons, Sullivan Street Tea & Spice Company, McNulty's, David's, Kusmi Tea, and Sun's Organic. It's always good to have a variety of teas for drinking and cooking.

New York City and its amazing variety of shops has become my inspiration for cooking. I never tire of adventuring around the city, gathering ingredients, and running home to cook, excited to experiment with my discoveries. My goal is to inspire you to venture around your home, whether it's here in New York or in the artisan shops of your own town. Which is not to say that you have to run around town like I do; this is what I love to do, so it's natural for me. If your area doesn't offer artisanal cheese, Indian spice shops, or other places I mention throughout the book, you can order online (web addresses on pages 193–203). I simply want to inspire you, whether you choose to spend a day seeking out ingredients or ordering them from the comforts of home. There are so many gifts and treasures to find at specialty food stores, and I don't want you to miss out on all their offerings. Plus, the people behind these stores love what they do and want to share their products.

Find more recipes and information about the New York City food scene on my website: newyorkcity.kitchen

STAPLE ITEMS FOR UNORDINARY COOKING

I've never been satisfied with regular ol' salt and pepper at the supermarket, or the dried herbs sitting in jars when fresh ones are so much tastier. My adventurous spirit has led me to find great salts, spices, butter, and olive oil with which to cook. I think great ingredients can turn a mediocre dish into something more. Here is a list of the staples I have on hand most of the time, and where I buy them. Even if you can't trek around New York City to gather these basic ingredients (which I do recommend if you live here or come to visit), you can easily order most of them online and have them delivered right to your door (web addresses on pages 193–203). That is, if you can't find them in your neighborhood stores.

Olive oil: There are so many places to get olive oil, but my favorite is the one from Frankies 457 Spuntino. It could be that this is a local restaurant I adore, but the incredible flavor is undeniable. I also buy olive oil from Il Buco Alimentari, Di Palo's, Eataly, and sometimes Dean & DeLuca.

Butter: Head to Zabar's for American (Keller's Plugrá), Dutch (Lurpak), or French (Beurre d'Echire) butter, to Eataly for Italian butter, and for locally made butter, visit Murray's Cheese or Saxelby Cheesemongers.

Salt: The Meadow, hands down, is the best place to buy salt, simply for their large collection of what was once thought of as a mundane ingredient. Here, you can get a wide variety of traditional sea salt, flaky salt, smoked salt, rock salt, Himalayan, grinder, cooking, curing, coarse, pickling, and brining salt—and even salt blocks.

Peppercorns: Although black peppercorns are the most popular, it's also nice to have pink and white peppercorns for certain recipes. Kalustyan's has a large selection, including black tellicherry, white, pink, and green, among other blends.

Spices: Kalustyan's is one of my favorite stores for spices from cardamom pods to Chinese five-spice powder. If you haven't been there, I highly suggest a visit. You'll be astounded at the variety of spices, not to mention a million other ingredients you didn't know you wanted. I also pick up spices at Spices and Tease in the Chelsea Market, Sahadi's, Patel Brothers, and Two for the Pot. La Boîte has some gorgeous blends. These are the spices I keep stocked most of the time: smoked paprika, Chinese five-spice, cardamom, cumin, coriander, garam masala, Sunny Paris from Penzeys Spices (mail order), za'atar, and shawarma.

Eggs: For local eggs, I visit the Union Square Greenmarket and other farmers' markets around the city. I love Tello's Green Farm or Wild Hive Farm, but any local farm will have eggs that are far superior to the supermarket brands. Honestly, there is no comparison.

Rice: White, brown, jasmine, long grain, short grain . . . there are so many varieties! Head to Hong Kong Supermarket for bulk rice shopping (jasmine, brown, and sushi) or Kalustyan's for more obscure types. I also pick up different types of grains from Eataly and Il Buco Alimentari.

Coffee: Coffee is my morning elixir, and I use it in a few of my recipes, too. For great coffee beans, head to Roasting Plant, where they roast coffee beans on site, or Stumptown, D'Amico Coffee, Blue Bottle, Brooklyn Roasting Company, and Porto Rico Importing.

Tea: While coffee is my morning drink, tea is my afternoon beverage. I also add tea to cupcakes and pound cakes. Harney & Sons in SoHo has so many wonderful choices that I can barely make up my mind; I love Brigitte's Blend for a brisk cup and the SoHo blend, which has coconut and vanilla overtones (so great with milk on a cold day). I also enjoy teas from Kusmi Tea and Mariage Frères.

Bread: I have not ventured into baking my own bread. Someday, I will. For now, I buy bread mostly at Maison Kayser, Balthazar, Amy's Bread, Bien Cuit, and Caputo Bakery. I love having bread around for snacking with cheese from, say, Murray's or Stinky Bklyn, and to eat with all the dips and stews included in this book.

Chocolate: I love baking with chocolate from Mast Brothers, Scharffen Berger, Jacques Torres, or L.A. Burdick. To nibble on while I'm at home cooking or writing, some of my favorite chocolates are from Kee's Chocolates. I also like the bars from Vosges Haut-Chocolat.

Other: On a regular basis, I also keep these items stocked: both red and white wine for cooking and drinking, tamarind, a variety of mustards from Maille (I love their mustards on tap!), local honey, citrus fruits, a variety of vinegars (balsamic, white, and rice wine), lemongrass, garlic, fresh ginger, Parmesan, onions, shallots, olives, scallions, saba, fish sauce, chili paste, sesame oil, miso, orange blossom water, rose water, fig jam, guava paste, saffron, and lots of spices.

A few helpful kitchen tools

No one wants a ton of extra kitchen tools sitting around causing clutter, but I swear by these few items.

KitchenAid mixer: great for cakes, pizza dough, whipped cream, cake batter, and more.

Immersion blender: for quick sauces.

Tiny food processor: I use this to chop garlic and onions, and I happen to have gotten a great one from Tupperware. It's not electronic, but works wonders on small ingredients.

Larger food processor: for dips, sauces, puréed soups, and more.

High-quality knives: I suggest Wüsthof and Korin, which sell professional cutlery from Germany and Japan.

Mortar and pestle: this is one of my favorite tools for crushing herbs, garlic, nuts, and more to make pastas and sauces. I love this one shown from Emile Henry.

Appetizers, Dips, and Party Food

For Impromptu Get-Togethers

I love to snack, but not on junk food. You'll never catch me buying potato chips or chemical-laden cheese doodles at the local bodega. But I do love nibbling throughout the day on cheese, flatbread with dips, grilled vegetables, and charcuterie. During hectic days, these "snacks," paired with a salad, turn into a meal. And they serve another purpose: when friends come over on a whim, you have something lovely to offer—alongside a glass of wine!

Roasted Red Pepper Spread

Serves 2–4

When my daughter was in kindergarten, I invited one of her friend's parents over for dinner. We became fast friends, I think in part, because of this spread. My favorite way to eat it is on grilled bread (alongside wine or coffee) and served with paella or bouillabaisse. You could roast your own red peppers or simply use a jar to make things easier.

1 (12-ounce) jar roasted red peppers (or roast 2 peppers
   on a cookie sheet in the oven at 400°F for
   15–20 minutes, then remove skin)
3 cloves garlic
1 cup panko bread crumbs
   or some stale bread, chopped
juice of 1 lemon
¼ cup parsley
½ teaspoon cayenne pepper
½ teaspoon dried ancho chile pepper, crumbled
½ teaspoon coarse salt
½ teaspoon freshly ground pepper
⅓ cup extra-virgin olive oil

Add all ingredients to a food processor or blender.
Combine until the spread is slightly coarse, not smooth.

QUICK TIP

I love keeping a few dips and spreads in my refrigerator. They're a nice addition to lunch with some fresh vegetables and flatbread, or even on their own for when friends visit. Speaking of flatbread, you could make your own, a laborious endeavor for sure, but there's no need when you have stores like Damascus Bakery and Kings Highway Bakery, both of which serve the freshest, fluffiest pita bread you'll ever taste.

Tzatziki

Serves 2–4

Of all the Greek dips, tzatziki is the most refreshing, and while you can certainly buy it at a store like Titan Foods in Astoria, it's actually very easy to make. Serve with vegetables and flatbread. It also makes a great sauce for meatballs, sandwiches, chicken, or fish.

2 cups plain yogurt
1 cucumber, peeled, chopped
3 cloves garlic

juice of 1 lemon
salt and freshly ground pepper, to taste
2 tablespoons fresh dill, plus more for garnish

Add all ingredients to a blender. Blend until smooth. Top with additional dill.

Olive Tapenade

Serves 2–4

Tapenade is a sublime and salty delight that pairs well with a glass of wine and some crunchy bread from, say, Bien Cuit or Caputo Bakery. You could also spread some on fish before baking.

2 cups olives, a mix of black and green
3 cloves garlic
2 teaspoons anchovy paste
1 tablespoon capers
1 tablespoon fresh basil

1 tablespoon fresh parsley
juice of 1 lemon (about 1 tablespoon)
1 tablespoon olive oil
1 teaspoon salt
1 teaspoon freshly ground black pepper

Add all ingredients to a food processor and blend until just combined. The tapenade should be slightly chunky.

Appetizers, Dips, and Party Food

Sweet Potato and Carrot Dip
with Nigella Seeds

Serves 2–4

Well-known in India, nigella seeds aren't a common spice, but you can find them in a spice shop like Kalustyan's. They most resemble black sesame seeds, which can be used as an alternative.

2 medium-sized sweet potatoes
2 carrots, peeled
¼ cup walnuts
2 teaspoons smoked paprika, divided
2 teaspoons cumin, divided
1 tablespoon olive oil, plus more for drizzling

2 cloves garlic
juice and zest of 1 lemon
salt and freshly ground pepper, to taste
2 chives, chopped
1 tablespoon nigella seeds (optional)
1 tablespoon fresh coriander or parsley

Preheat oven to 450°F. Use a fork to poke holes in the sweet potatoes. Then, place the sweet potatoes and carrots in a baking dish. Drizzle the potatoes with olive oil and roast for 45 minutes.

In a separate bowl, toss the walnuts with one teaspoon each of smoked paprika and cumin. In a skillet over medium heat, heat up the walnuts until browned. Set aside. Once cooled off, chop or mash in a mortar and pestle.

When the sweet potatoes and carrots are done and out of the oven, cut the sweet potatoes in half and let cool for about 10 minutes. Remove the skin.

Place the sweet potatoes, carrots, 1 tablespoon olive oil, 1 teaspoon each of paprika and cumin, garlic, lemon juice and zest, salt, and pepper in a blender and mix until combined. Stir in the chives. Top with prepared walnuts, nigella seeds, fresh herbs, and a dash of olive oil.

Miso-Honey Eggplant Dip

Serves 2–4

The wonderful sweet-salty-nutty flavors of miso pair well with eggplant. Serve with rice crackers or sliced vegetables.

QUICK TIP

I like to visit Spices and Tease in Chelsea Market when I'm in the neighborhood to pick up one of my go-to spice blends: Japanese seven-spice; a combination of orange peel, black, white, and toasted sesame seeds, cayenne, ginger, Szechuan pepper, and nori. You can sprinkle it on so many dishes from vegetables to seafood to eggs to noodle dishes. Here it adds some crunch and heat to roasted eggplant.

2 small-to-medium eggplants, halved lengthwise
1 tablespoon sesame oil
2 tablespoons miso
2 tablespoons rice vinegar
1 tablespoon soy sauce
2 tablespoons honey
2 teaspoons Japanese seven-spice or sesame seeds, divided
2 scallions, chopped

Place eggplant halves on a cookie sheet and rub with sesame oil. Place under the broiler in your oven for about 5 minutes. Turn the eggplant over and broil for another 5 minutes. Then, turn over again so that the fleshy side is facing up. In a separate bowl, combine miso with rice vinegar. Add soy sauce, honey, and 1 teaspoon of Japanese seven-spice or sesame seeds. Mix until combined. Spread over the eggplant flesh and broil for about 30 minutes, until soft. Remove from oven and cool. Remove flesh and mash until smooth. Top with 1 additional teaspoon of Japanese seven-spice and chopped scallions.

Mini Greek Meatballs

Serves 2–4

Having a young daughter who loves meatballs, I've made many varieties. What's great about mini meatballs is that they can be eaten on their own as an appetizer, in a sandwich for lunch, or as a main course along with some side dishes. Although I recommend pan frying these, you can also bake them at 400°F for about 15 minutes.

1 pound ground beef
¼ cup feta cheese
1 tablespoon oregano
¼ cup tzatziki, plus more for serving
zest of 1 lemon

1 egg
¼ cup bread crumbs
salt and freshly ground pepper, to taste
¼ cup olive or vegetable oil

Place the ground beef in a bowl. Break up with a fork. Add the remaining ingredients except oil and combine until well blended. Heat oil in a skillet over medium heat. Roll the meat mixture into small balls, about 1-inch thick. Place in the pan and cook until done, rolling them around in the pan so that the meat is cooked evenly throughout, about 5 to 6 minutes altogether. Serve with tzatziki.

MINI ITALIAN MEATBALLS

Replace feta, oregano, tzatziki, and lemon with: ¼ cup Parmesan, 1 tablespoon basil, and ¼ cup tomato sauce. Serve with tomato sauce.

MINI VIETNAMESE MEATBALLS

Replace feta, oregano, tzatziki, and lemon with: 2 tablespoons shredded carrots, 2 tablespoons fish sauce, 2 tablespoons sriracha, 1 tablespoon chopped fresh mint, 1 tablespoon chopped fresh cilantro, and 2 cloves minced garlic.

MINI TUNISIAN MEATBALLS

Replace feta, oregano, tzatziki, and lemon with: 2 cloves minced garlic, 2 teaspoons harissa paste, and 2 teaspoons fenugreek seeds.

MINI CARIBBEAN MEATBALLS

Replace feta, oregano, tzatziki, and lemon with: 1 chopped Scotch bonnet chili pepper, 1 tablespoon jerk spice, and 2 tablespoons chopped scallions.

Burrata with Grapes and Pistachios

Serves 4

Burrata is a wonderfully creamy form of mozzarella. I was inspired to serve the burrata with grapes from an appetizer I enjoyed at one of my go-to neighborhood restaurants, Frankies 457 Spuntino. Frankies also sells stellar olive oil, which I recommend drizzling over the cheese.

Several arugula leaves
8 ounces burrata
¼ cup small seedless grapes (Champagne grapes are the perfect size, but if you find larger grapes, halve or quarter them)

zest of 1 lemon
saba or sweet balsamic vinegar, to drizzle over the cheese
extra-virgin olive oil, to drizzle over the cheese
2 tablespoons pistachios, ground

Arrange arugula leaves on a plate and place burrata on top. Add grapes and lemon zest. Drizzle with saba and olive oil, then top with ground pistachios. Serve immediately.

Papaya White Bean Dip

Serves 4

Combining papaya, white beans, and jalapeño with a dash of mint and honey is a combination that works well with chopped vegetables or crackers.

2 cups canned white beans
1 cup fresh papaya, peeled and cut into chunks
2 teaspoons jalapeño pepper, chopped
2 tablespoons fresh ginger, chopped
2 tablespoons honey
2 tablespoons olive oil

zest of 2 limes
2 tablespoons fresh mint
1 teaspoon salt
1 teaspoon freshly ground pepper
2 tablespoons scallions, chopped
2 teaspoons sesame seeds (optional)

If you are using dried white beans, you'll have to soak them in water ahead of time, ideally overnight, then boil until soft. This is preferable, but you can use canned white beans if time is an issue. Then, add all the ingredients, except for the scallions and sesame seeds, in a small food processor. Or, you can use an immersion blender or simply blend with a large fork. Blend until combined. Top with scallions and sesame seeds.

Grilled Halloumi
with Peppadew Peppers, Olives, and Pine Nuts

Halloumi is a tangy Mediterranean cheese made of milk from both goats and sheep. It can be a challenge to find, but Titan Foods in Astoria always has it in stock. Serve about 8 ounces of halloumi cheese per person.

½ cup arugula leaves
¼ cup mint
1 clove garlic
2 tablespoons olive oil, divided
8 ounces halloumi cheese
¼ cup Peppadew peppers, chopped

¼ cup mixed olives, chopped
1 tablespoon capers
½ teaspoon freshly ground black pepper
1 tablespoon fresh chives, chopped
1 tablespoon fresh oregano, chopped
1 tablespoon pine nuts

Combine arugula leaves, mint, and garlic. Either in a small food processor or a mortar and pestle, combine them until broken up. Add in 1 tablespoon olive oil and combine until you get a pesto-like consistency.

Next, heat remaining 1 tablespoon olive oil in a grill pan over medium heat. Slice cheese into thick slices. Grill for about 1 minute on each side. Place on top of arugula leaves. Top with Peppadew peppers, olives, and capers. Drizzle with arugula-mint combination, sprinkle with pepper, and top with chopped chives, oregano, and pine nuts. Serve immediately.

Cheese and Charcuterie Platter

This isn't a recipe, but rather inspiration to serve a cheese and charcuterie platter the next time you're having friends over. It's always a good idea to have a mix of different types of cheese—cow, sheep, goat, for example—and of varying textures. For meat, always get a mix, too, for different textures and flavors.

See the next page for three charcuterie* and five cheese** recommendations I picked up at Stinky Bklyn.

WHERE TO BUY CHEESE AND CHARCUTERIE

Astoria Bier and Cheese
Artisanal Fromagerie, Bistro and Premium Cheese
Bedford Cheese Shop
Beecher's
Bklyn Larder
Despaña
Eataly
Formaggio Kitchen
Ideal Cheese Shop
Lucy's Whey
Milk and Hops
Murray's Cheese
The Ploughman
Saxelby Cheesemongers
Stinky Bklyn

QUICK TIP

Serve your cheese and charcuterie with a few accoutrements, including Dijon mustard from Maille Mustard, honey with truffles from Urbani Truffles, orange saffron cardamom marmalade from Eat This, and some preserves that you like, perhaps peach or cherry.

---

*Charcuterie: 1. Larchmont bresaola (air-dried salted beef); 2. speck (smoked proscuitto); 3. spicy soppressata (Italian dry salami).

**Cheese: 4. Flory's Truckle (an old-world cheddar from Milton Creamery in Milton, Iowa); 5. Rogue River Blue (a cow's milk from Central Point); 6. Mahón (a cow's milk cheese from Minorca, Spain); 7. Stawley (a raw goat's milk cheese from Hill Farm Dairy in Somerset, England); 8. Délice de Bourgogne (a pasteurized cow's milk from Burgundy, France).

1.

2.

3.

4.

5.

6.

7.

Classic Pizza

Makes 2 (14-inch) pizzas

My daughter and I have our ritual pizza-and-movie-night nearly every Friday. While it might seem crazy to make pizza at home when you live in New York City, the land of a million pizza shops, there's something satisfying about the experience of making your own dough, using cheese that you've watched being made at say, Eataly or Casa Della Mozzarella, and picking your own toppings. You can use a regular cookie sheet or a pizza stone like the one shown from Emile Henry.

For the dough
2 packages yeast
2 cups warm (not hot!) water
2 teaspoons salt
4 cups bread or all-purpose flour

For the sauce
2 cups tomato sauce
2 cloves garlic, minced
1 teaspoon sugar
1 teaspoon fresh oregano, chopped
Salt and freshly ground pepper, to taste

For the cheese
2–3 slices muenster cheese, broken up into pieces
2 ounces mozzarella cheese, shredded

Prepare the dough ahead of time. I usually make it the morning of the day I plan on making the pizza. In a large bowl or in a KitchenAid mixer, combine yeast with warm water (be sure water isn't too hot!) and stir to combine. Add salt then slowly add the flour (1 cup at a time) and combine. If you're using a mixer, use the dough hook and cover the top of the bowl before mixing so the flour doesn't fly out. On medium speed, mix the flour with the yeast mixture. Remove the bowl from the mixer, cover it with a kitchen towel, and let rise for at least 4 hours or until ready to make.

Preheat oven to 425°F. When the dough has risen and you're ready to roll it out, clear a fairly large area on your counter or use a large wooden cutting board. Add some flour and/or cornmeal to the cutting board so that the dough doesn't stick to the surface. Keep extra flour or cornmeal nearby; if the dough is sticky, you'll want to add more while rolling it out. Split the dough into two mounds and take one mound, cover with flour, and start pressing until it gets flat. Then, use a rolling pin to roll it into a circle or desired shape. Make the tomato sauce by combining all ingredients listed. Spoon sauce over the dough, spreading it around the dough. Then, place pieces of muenster cheese on top of the sauce. Place mozzarella around the pizza and any toppings you like on the pizza. Bake for about 10 minutes or until cheese melts and is slightly bubbly. Remove from oven, then top with slivers of basil. I use scissors and cut the pieces on top of the pizza. Repeat the process for the second pizza.

TOPPINGS TO CONSIDER

Soppressata: I like to buy this from Italian specialty shops like Di Palo's Fine Foods or Teitel Brothers. Artisanal brands like Olli and La Quercia, which are often sold at gourmet shops and cheese stores, are also a good choice.

Basil: I used to put basil on the pizza before placing it in the oven, but I started adding it after the pizza comes out of the oven after seeing it done that way at Di Fara Pizza in Brooklyn.

Truffle Pizza

2 (14-inch) pizzas

If you love mushroom pizza, why not elevate the experience and opt for black or white truffles? I recommend tomato sauce with truffles from Urbani Truffles, who provide many NYC-area restaurants with this elegant mushroom. Top your pizza with shaved Urbani fresh truffles for an extra special treat.

Pizza dough (see recipe on page 33)
2 cans Tomatoes and Truffles from Urbani Truffles
8 slices Fontina cheese

1 ounce cremini mushrooms, sliced
1 small truffle, shaved (optional)
¼ cup freshly grated Parmesan

Make and roll out the dough as described in the classic pizza recipe (page 33). Place on cookie sheet or pizza stone. Top each pizza with 1 can of Tomatoes and Truffles. Top with slices of Fontina cheese. Place mushrooms on the pizza. Top with shaved truffles and grated Parmesan. Bake in the oven for 10 minutes or until cheese melts and is bubbly.

Mussels
in Garlic White Wine Sauce

Serves 2–4

Mussels are a great dish to serve at a party—or even for a weeknight dinner, paired with a salad. Be sure to serve with a crunchy bread like sourdough or Caputo Bakery's jalapeño cheddar bread (only available on the weekends) for dipping into the broth. Or serve grilled bread with the red pepper spread on page 17.

2 tablespoons olive oil
1 shallot, chopped
4 cloves garlic, minced
2 cups white wine
1 cup chicken broth
1 tablespoon herbes de Provence

1 teaspoon salt
2 teaspoons freshly ground pepper
1 pound mussels, cleaned and scrubbed
2 tablespoons parsley, coriander, or tarragon, chopped

In a large covered pot, heat olive oil over medium heat. Add the shallot and sauté until translucent. Add the garlic and continue to sauté, stirring for 1 to 2 minutes. Add the wine and chicken broth. Add the spices. Bring to a boil, then simmer for about 3 to 4 minutes. Finally, add the mussels and cover. When the mussels open, they're ready. This only takes a couple of minutes. Top with chopped fresh parsley, coriander, or tarragon.

MUSSELS IN SPICY TOMATO SAUCE

Follow the same directions, omitting the herbes de Provence. Add 4 Roma tomatoes, chopped. Add ¼ cup sun-dried tomatoes, chopped. Add 1 tablespoon crushed chili pepper. Top with 2 tablespoons chopped oregano.

MUSSELS IN LIME COCONUT MILK

Follow the same directions, omitting the herbes de Provence. Instead of wine, substitute 2 cans of coconut milk. Add the juice of 4 limes, then toss in the limes. Top with 1 tablespoon chopped mint and 1 tablespoon chopped Thai basil.

Soups, Stews, and Salads

When Something Different Is in Order

After a long day, there's nothing better than a salad or stew with a glass of wine or seltzer. Nibble on some flatbread or grab a baguette to dip into the broths of your favorite soups and stews. Toss some za'atar over yogurt with a drizzle of olive oil, or sprinkle some nigella seeds over hunks of feta or goat cheese. All of these can be served along with salad and soup for what I consider a complete meal.

And please, make your own salad dressings—it's something I wish everyone would do because, honestly, I haven't come across a supermarket dressing that beats the ones you can so easily make at home. If you keep ingredients like olive oil, vinegars, mustard, garlic, spices, and herbs stocked regularly, you can easily whip up a dressing. It's fun to experiment—and you'll never have to buy a store-bought dressing again.

Beet and Feta Salad
with Coriander-Orange Vinaigrette

Serves 2–4

Don't buy the dried, crumbled (dare I say bland?) feta at the supermarket. For fresh feta, head to a cheese store, or preferably, to a Greek market like Titan Foods in Astoria. They sell many different types of tangy feta—and you can taste them to find your favorite.

For the dressing
2 tablespoons olive oil
2 tablespoons fresh orange juice
1 tablespoon shallot, minced
2 teaspoons ground coriander
2 teaspoons ground black pepper
1 teaspoon coarse salt

For the salad
2 large beets, roasted, cubed
1 small red onion (⅓ cup), thinly sliced
¼ pound feta
1 small bunch fresh dill
1 tablespoon pine nuts
orange segments, to garnish
olives, to garnish
ground pistachios, to garnish

Add all dressing ingredients to a glass jar with a cover (or a bowl). Shake or whisk until combined. Arrange beets in a bowl and top with onion. Spoon dressing over the beets and onions, then top with feta, dill, and pine nuts. Garnish with orange segments, olives, and ground pistachios.

Potato-Dill Soup
with Truffles

Serves 2–4

Earthy truffles partnered with potatoes are a delightful match—humble potatoes are transformed with the woodsy flavor of truffles.

QUICK TIP

Truffles are definitely a treat, but so worth it on occasion. You can get truffles at most high-end markets or head to where many New York City chefs get theirs: Urbani Truffles. You can visit their shop or order online. Although fresh truffles are optimal, I keep a frozen one in my freezer so I can shave it onto a dish whenever the craving occurs.

4 medium potatoes, chopped
1 large white or yellow onion, chopped
4 cups chicken stock
salt and pepper, to taste
2 cups buttermilk
fresh dill
smoked salt (I recommend the smoked salt at The Meadow)
black or white truffle shavings, to garnish

In a medium saucepan, add potatoes and onion and cover with chicken stock. Season with salt and pepper. Bring to a boil, then lower heat and simmer until potatoes are soft. Once the potatoes are soft, add the stock/potatoes/onion mixture to a food processor. Add buttermilk and fresh dill. Blend until combined. Serve in individual bowls. Sprinkle with smoked salt and a few pieces of shaved truffle.

Truffles from Urbani Truffles

Fennel Orange Salad

Serves 2–4

Fennel and orange served together are a Sicilian specialty. If you have a mandoline, this is the time to break it out for see-through thin fennel and red onion. But if you don't, an extra sharp knife (I like those from Wüsthof and Korin) works well, too.

1 fennel bulb, thinly sliced
2 oranges (1 for orange segments, 1 for fresh juice)
½ cup red onion, thinly sliced
¼ cup olives, chopped

¼ cup olive oil
1 clove garlic, minced
1 tablespoon fennel fronds, chopped
¼ teaspoon salt
¼ teaspoon freshly ground pepper

Combine fennel, orange segments from 1 orange, onion, and olives. In a separate small bowl, combine fresh orange juice from 1 orange, olive oil, garlic, fennel fronds, and salt and pepper. Mix until combined. Drizzle over salad.

Asian-Inspired Gazpacho

Serves 2–4

I've reinvented gazpacho, a cold tomato-based soup from Spain, and added Asian-inspired ingredients to this recipe for a refreshing twist. Serve with scallion pancakes that you can pick up at Asian specialty stores like Fei Long Supermarket in Brooklyn or Hong Kong Supermarket in Manhattan.

5–6 Roma tomatoes
¼ cup green pepper, chopped
½ cucumber, peeled, chopped
2 teaspoons sesame oil

2 tablespoons rice vinegar
1 tablespoon soy sauce
2 scallions, chopped, divided (1 stalk for the soup, 1 stalk to garnish)

Combine all ingredients in a blender or food processor and mix until combined. Garnish with chopped scallion. Serve with scallion pancakes.

Despaña in SoHo

Clam, Saffron, and Chorizo Stew

Serves 4

Chorizo adds a ton of flavor to tomato-based dishes, and I especially love it paired with clams. Head to Despaña in SoHo for their outstanding chorizo. Serve this as is or over pasta, perhaps fresh linguine or tagliatelle from D. Coluccio & Sons.

2 tablespoons olive oil
2 ounces hard chorizo, chopped
½ cup shallot, chopped
3 cloves garlic, minced
4 Roma tomatoes, chopped
1 cup white wine

1 pinch saffron
zest and juice of 1 orange
1 teaspoon salt
1½ teaspoons freshly ground black pepper
16–20 clams in the shell (littlenecks are great!)
1 tablespoon parsley, chopped

Heat olive oil in a stew pan over medium heat. Add the chorizo and sauté until crisp, about 2 to 3 minutes. Add shallot and sauté until translucent. Add the garlic and sauté for 1 minute. Add the chopped tomatoes, then the wine. Add the pinch of saffron, orange zest and juice, and salt and pepper. Bring to a boil, then lower heat and simmer for 3 minutes. Add the clams and cover. The dish is ready when the clams open, about 6 to 8 minutes; discard any that haven't. Place clams and sauce in a large bowl or serve right out of the pan. Top with parsley.

Smoked Oyster Chowder

Serves 2–4

Fresh oysters, which I love, don't require any sort of recipe, which is why I didn't include them in this book. Instead, I've shared a chowder made with smoked oysters; they come in a can, but the delicious smoky flavor is well worth it!

4 cups whole milk
4–5 pieces bacon, cooked, crumbled
¼ cup flour
1 teaspoon smoked salt (I recommend Red Alder from The Meadow)
2 teaspoons freshly ground or white black pepper

1 (3-ounce) can smoked oysters
¼ cup brandy
½ cup celery, chopped
1 teaspoon crushed chipotle pepper or cayenne
1 tablespoon thyme, chopped

In a saucepan, heat the milk over low heat. In a separate large saucepan with high edges, cook the bacon over medium heat until crisp. Remove the bacon and pour out most of the bacon fat, leaving about 1 to 2 tablespoons. Add flour, smoked salt, and pepper, and stir quickly with the bacon fat to form a paste. Add in the canned oysters with liquid. Add in brandy, then celery, and crushed pepper or cayenne. Stir, then simmer until celery is soft, about 3 to 4 minutes. Add the warm milk and simmer for another 2 to 3 minutes. Remove from heat and stir in bacon pieces and fresh thyme.

Soups, Stews, and Salads

Salmon and Watercress Salad with Maple-Mustard Vinaigrette

Serves 4

Combine mustard, maple, and crushed chili peppers for a sweet and spicy salad dressing that complements the peppery watercress.

For the dressing
1 teaspoon Dijon mustard (I recommend Maille's
    Rich Country mustard)
¼ teaspoon crushed chili pepper
⅓ cup maple syrup
½ cup olive oil
½ teaspoon salt
½ teaspoon pepper

For the salad
2 bunches watercress
1 cup cooked corn
2 (8-ounce) pieces honey-maple salmon (recipe
    on page 87)

Combine all ingredients for the dressing in a glass container. I like using a mason jar. Cover and shake vigorously until combined. Arrange watercress in a bowl, removing some of the thick stems. Add the corn and pieces of broken up salmon. Drizzle with salad dressing.

Squash Soup
with Ginger and Leeks

Serves 4

On a cozy fall evening, make this creamy squash soup that has a touch of heat from the ginger and smokiness from the ancho chili. Serve with sweet potato dip (page 21) and flatbread.

2 teaspoons butter
1 cup leeks, halved, sliced, plus extra for garnish
1 (1-inch) piece ginger
1 pound squash, cut into chunks
1 cup white wine
2 cups chicken or vegetable stock

1 teaspoon salt
1 teaspoon freshly ground black pepper
1 teaspoon crushed ancho chile pepper
¼ teaspoon smoked paprika
⅓ cup milk or cream
2 teaspoons pumpkin seeds

Heat butter in a saucepan over low-medium heat. Add the leeks and sauté, while stirring, for about 2 minutes. Add the ginger and sauté for another 2 minutes. Add the squash, wine, stock, salt, pepper, ancho chile pepper, and smoked paprika. Raise heat to high and bring to a boil. Then lower heat and simmer until the squash is cooked, about 8 to 10 minutes. Remove from heat and add to a food processor or blender. Blend until combined. Then add milk or cream and blend until smooth. Garnish with pumpkin seeds and chopped leeks.

Chicken, Chickpeas, and Chorizo Stew with Lime Yogurt

Serves 4

This is another stew in which I sauté chorizo as a flavorful base. The lime yogurt adds a welcome tang to this piquant dish. You could also substitute the limes for orange, which used to be my go-to combination (until I tried it with lime). Feel free to add in your favorite grain, perhaps buckwheat or barley, for a heartier dish.

2 tablespoons olive oil
2 ounces hard chorizo, chopped
6 ounces chicken breast
½ cup shallot, chopped
3 cloves garlic, minced
2 Roma tomatoes, chopped
1 tablespoon tomato paste
1 cup chickpeas*

1 cup white wine
1 pinch saffron
zest and juice of 2 limes, divided
1 teaspoon salt
1½ teaspoons freshly ground black pepper
1 cup plain yogurt
2 tablespoons parsley, chopped

Heat olive oil in a stew pan over medium heat. Add the chorizo and sauté 2 minutes. Add the chicken and sear for about 3 minutes on each side. Remove the chicken; let sit for 5 minutes, then cut into small pieces. Add shallot and sauté until translucent. Add the garlic and sauté for another minute. Add the tomatoes, tomato paste, chickpeas, and wine. Add the pinch of saffron, zest and juice from 1 lime, and salt and pepper. Bring to a boil, then add the chicken pieces. Lower heat, cover, and simmer for about 10 to 15 minutes, adding more wine if needed. In a separate bowl, mix yogurt together with additional lime zest and juice. When the stew is ready, serve with a dollop of yogurt and parsley.

*Use dried chickpeas, preferably, that have been soaked in water overnight.

Soups, Stews, and Salads

Arugula
with Shawarma-Spiced Almonds, Goat Cheese, and Miso Vinaigrette

Serves 4

Miso vinaigrette is one of my favorite dressings. Its umami flavor pairs nicely with spiced almonds and goat cheese. You can buy miso paste at most Asian markets, including Sunrise Mart, a Japanese market. Get a nice tangy goat cheese for this salad, perhaps some Bucheron from Murray's Cheese.

¾ cup almonds
1 tablespoon shawarma spice, available at Kalustyan's and online at Pereg Natural Foods
1 tablespoon olive oil
2 tablespoons miso paste
2 tablespoons rice vinegar
¾ cup canola oil

1 tablespoon honey
2 teaspoons fresh lemon juice
2 teaspoons freshly ground black pepper
1 tablespoon scallions, chopped
2 teaspoons white or black sesame seeds
4 cups arugula
4–6 ounces goat cheese

Toss almonds, shawarma spice, and olive oil in a bowl. In a small skillet over medium heat, sauté the almonds until browned. Remove from pan. Let cool, then crush in a mortar and pestle.

In a separate bowl, combine miso paste and rice vinegar and let stand for 2 to 3 minutes. Stir until combined. Add in the remaining ingredients except arugula and goat cheese. Stir or whisk until combined. Arrange arugula in a large salad bowl. Drizzle the miso dressing over the greens. Crumble goat cheese and toss the crushed nuts and additional shawarma spice, if you like, over the salad.

Curry Cod Stew

Serves 4

If you like ordering takeout because you think you can't make curries at home, try this tangy, fiery Thai dish and skip the delivery service. Imagine fish and string beans (or make your own protein and vegetable combination) simmering in the sweet-spicy coconut curry . . . it's a keeper. Add more chili paste if you like it hot, and serve with your favorite rice (I recommend jasmine or sushi rice).

1 tablespoon olive oil
½ cup white or yellow onion, chopped
2 garlic cloves, chopped
2 teaspoons jalapeño pepper, minced
1 green or red pepper, chopped
1 cup green beans, destemmed, chopped into 1-inch pieces
1 carrot, sliced
1 can coconut milk
1 cup broth or dashi
2 teaspoons curry powder
2 teaspoons Thai chili paste
½ teaspoon salt
1 teaspoon freshly ground black pepper
2 (6-ounce) cod fillets
1 tablespoon Thai basil, chopped

QUICK TIP

Thai chili paste, or Nam Prik Pao, is a smoky, sweet, tart, tangy mixture of chili peppers, onion, garlic, tamarind, and sugar. It's a definite must-have if you like Thai flavors. You can buy Thai chili paste at a store like Bangkok Center Grocery in Manhattan's Chinatown.

Heat olive oil in a saucepan over medium heat. Add the onion and sauté until translucent. Add the garlic and jalapeño pepper; stir. Add the pepper, green beans, and carrot; stir. Add coconut milk, broth or dashi, curry powder, chili paste, salt, and pepper. Stir until combined and simmer for about 5 minutes. Add the cod and simmer on low heat for 7 to 9 minutes. Garnish with Thai basil and serve with rice.

Fresh Fig and Mixed Green Salad with Saba

Serves 4

Fresh figs are in season at the beginning of the summer and often through the beginning of fall, when they're ubiquitous at every fruit stand. I like getting them at the Union Square Greenmarket or Three Guys from Brooklyn, which is a wonderful open air market, perfect for stocking up on fresh fruits and vegetables. Saba, a vinegar made from the must of Trebbiano grapes, is one of my main staples. It has a caramelized sweetness and tartness at the same time.

4 cups mixed greens
½ cup radicchio, chopped
6–8 figs, quartered

4 ounces Parmesan, chopped
saba, for drizzling
salt and freshly ground black pepper, to taste

Arrange greens in 4 bowls. Distribute radicchio onto each plate, then figs, then Parmesan. Drizzle with saba and sprinkle with salt and pepper.

Kale Salad with Dates and Ricotta Salata

Serves 4

Ricotta salata—basically hard-pressed ricotta cheese—is salty and milky, a welcome contrast to the bitterness of kale and the sweetness of dates.

1 lemon, juiced
½ cup extra-virgin olive oil
2 teaspoons red wine vinegar
2 teaspoons herbes de Provence
1 teaspoon salt (I recommend a French Fleur de Sel from The Meadow)

1 teaspoon freshly ground black pepper
4 cups kale, small chopped
1 cup dates, deseeded, chopped
4 ounces ricotta salata, chopped

Combine lemon juice, olive oil, vinegar, herbes de Provence, salt, and pepper in a jar. Whisk or shake, covered, until combined. Arrange kale in a large bowl. Drizzle with dressing. Top with dates and ricotta salata.

Soups, Stews, and Salads

Tomato, Purslane, and Sumac Salad

Serves 4

Sumac is a Middle Eastern spice that's sweet, citrusy, and tart. Its gorgeous scarlet color makes it a great spice for dusting over salads. You can buy it at any Middle Eastern grocery store, including Sahadi's.

1 clove garlic, minced
1 tablespoon shallot, chopped
2 teaspoons sumac
1 teaspoon za'atar
¾ cup olive oil
2 tablespoons fresh orange juice
½ teaspoon salt
1 teaspoon freshly ground pepper
2 cups purslane lettuce, chopped
½ pound cherry tomatoes, halved or ½ pound heirloom tomatoes
1 tablespoon pistachios, crushed

QUICK TIP

"Sahadi's in Brooklyn is my go-to place for a lot of Mediterranean and Middle Eastern products and flavors. I get inspired when cruising the aisles."

—Jacques Torres

Combine garlic, shallot, sumac, za'atar, olive oil, orange juice, salt, and pepper in a container with a lid. Shake until combined. Place purslane and tomatoes in a bowl. Drizzle with dressing. Sprinkle with crushed pistachios.

Don't Compromise on Flavor

Weekday Dinners

During the week, life gets busy. Trust me, I know how it is. It can be a challenge when you love food so much, yet don't have hours and hours to make meals you love. But there's no reason to compromise on an enjoyable meal. This chapter includes recipes that are easy to make yet elegant and full of flavor for those who crave something tasty without having to put in a lot of time and effort. Though admittedly, you will have to spend *some* time in the kitchen. But look at cooking as an act of love. When I am feeling stressed, that's how I see it: I am nurturing my loved ones and preparing them a home cooked meal as an expression of my love. I've created dishes that won't take hours to make, but will satiate your appetite for something a bit out of the ordinary.

I find that if I have all the ingredients at home, half the battle is over; it's the planning and shopping that takes most of the effort. I recommend making a list of everything you need for the week and getting it all on one day (except for fish, which you may want to buy the day of or the day before you're going to make it). The following recipes aren't difficult to put together, yet they offer a pleasurable eating experience for when time is of the essence.

Polenta
with Fontina and Wild Mushrooms

Serves 4

Creamy polenta and wild mushrooms simmered in red wine are a comforting combination. You can serve this as a main or side dish. Use a mix of whatever mushrooms you like. I usually turn to wild mushrooms, including shiitake, oyster, chanterelle, and one of my favorites: chicken of the woods, which has a meaty texture akin to chicken.

For the polenta
4 cups water
1 teaspoon salt
1 cup polenta
½ cup milk
½ cup grated Fontina
2 tablespoons butter

For the mushrooms
2 teaspoons butter
1 tablespoon olive oil
1 medium shallot, chopped
1 pound wild mushrooms
salt and freshly ground pepper, to taste
2 tablespoons fresh thyme, chopped, plus extra for garnish
1 tablespoon fresh sage, chopped, plus extra for garnish
½ –1 cup dry red wine

Boil salted water in a saucepan over high heat. Lower heat and add in polenta, whisking until smooth. Simmer for about 15 minutes, stirring frequently. Remove from heat and whisk in milk, Fontina, and butter. Heat butter and olive oil in a skillet over medium heat. Add shallot and sauté for about 2 minutes. Add mushrooms and stir. Add salt, pepper, thyme and sage. Then, add ½ cup of wine and simmer for 5 minutes, adding more wine if necessary. Continue to simmer for another 3 to 4 minutes. Pour mushrooms over polenta, sprinkle with fresh herbs, and serve.

Don't Compromise on Flavor

Chilean Sea Bass
with Papaya Ponzu Sauce

Serves 4

Chilean sea bass is a melt-in-your-mouth buttery fish that lends itself to the sweet-spicy flavors of the papaya ponzu sauce. Thai basil, with its licorice flavors and spiciness, is one of my favorite herbs, and I just love it paired with the sweetness of papaya. This is a weeknight meal you'll want to make again.

2 tablespoons ponzu sauce
¼ teaspoon crushed chili pepper
1 teaspoon sesame oil
¾ cup fresh papaya, thinly sliced or small chopped
½ red onion, sliced

2 teaspoons Thai basil, chopped
4 (6-ounce) Chilean sea bass fillets
1 teaspoon salt
1 teaspoon freshly ground pepper
1 tablespoon olive oil

Start with the sauce. Combine the ponzu with chili pepper and sesame oil. Add the papaya, onion, and Thai basil; stir to combine. Pat the fish dry and place on a cutting board. Season with salt and pepper. Add olive oil to a skillet over medium heat. When the pan is hot, add the fish, flesh-side down, and cook without moving the fish for 3 to 4 minutes until a nice crust forms. Turn the fish over and cook for an additional 2 to 3 minutes. Top with papaya ponzu sauce.

QUICK TIP

Ponzu is an Asian sauce with citrus overtones, perfect for seafood dishes. You can find ponzu sauce at any Asian market, including Fei Long Supermarket, Han Ah Reum Asian Mart, Hong Kong Supermarket, Inthira Thai Market, and Sunrise Mart.

QUICK TIP

"I love Han Ah Reum Asian Mart in Koreatown. It's your one-stop shop for all things Korean and Japanese. You gotta love a place that carries fifteen different kinds of dried squid."
—Jason Weiner, chef and owner of Almond and L&W Oyster Co.

Quick Korean Short Ribs

Serves 4

You'll want to make the marinade ahead of time for this dish, either the night before or the morning of the day you make it. Once you remove the marinated meat from the refrigerator, the dish takes just minutes to make.

½ cup dark soy sauce
½ cup regular soy sauce
1 tablespoon sugar
2 teaspoons rice vinegar
2 teaspoons sriracha

1 clove garlic, minced
1 tablespoon fresh mint, chopped
2 teaspoons freshly ground black pepper
3 tablespoons scallions, chopped, divided
2 pounds short ribs

Combine all the ingredients in a bowl, except for 1 tablespoon of the scallions and the short ribs. Place the short ribs in a shallow dish and pour the sauce over the meat. Refrigerate anywhere from 1 hour to overnight; the flavors will meld more the longer you marinate the meat, but if you're in somewhat of a rush, an hour will definitely suffice. When you're ready to cook, remove the meat from the refrigerator and let it sit for about 1 minute. Fire up a grill or heat a grill pan over medium-high heat. Grill the meat for about 4 minutes per side. Garnish with additional chopped scallions.

Walnut-Crusted Scallops
with Brown Butter Grapefruit Sauce

Serves 4

Scallops are surprisingly easy to make, and with walnuts, brown butter, and grapefruit this dish is a lovely flavor combination of sweet, citrusy, and nutty.

1 large grapefruit, halved

⅓ cup unsalted butter, plus 1 tablespoon

1 tablespoon shallot, minced

¼ cup white wine

salt and freshly ground pepper, about ½ teaspoon each,
    plus more for seasoning

¼ cup walnuts

16–20 large sea scallops

1 tablespoon fresh tarragon, chopped

2 teaspoons nigella seeds (optional)

QUICK TIP

There are so many wonderful fishmongers in New York. My go-to spot is Fish Tales in Brooklyn. I also frequent Sea Breeze Fish Market in Bensonhurst and Wild Edibles in Midtown.

Zest ½ grapefruit. Juice that same side of the grapefruit. Remove all grapefruit segments from the other half. Start browning ⅓ cup butter in a skillet over medium heat. Add the shallot. Swirl the butter around the pan and continue to cook the butter until it turns brown. Add grapefruit juice and stir, then add white wine, salt, and pepper, and stir some more. Add grapefruit segments and stir for another minute, then remove from heat and cover.

Crush the walnuts in a mortar and pestle until fine. Season the scallops with salt and pepper, then cover with walnuts. Heat up the remaining butter in a separate skillet over medium heat. When the butter is hot, add the scallops, walnut-side down, and cook for 3 minutes on each side without moving them so a crust can form. Once the scallops are done, place on individual plates and drizzle with the grapefruit sauce. Sprinkle with tarragon and nigella seeds.

Seared Tamari-Orange Scallops

Serves 4

Tamari, orange, and sesame seeds evoke a traditional Chinese sauce for breaded chicken, yet this one calls for Lillet, which adds a bit of French flair.

16–20 sea scallops
½ teaspoon salt
½ teaspoon freshly ground pepper
2 teaspoons black and white sesame seeds, plus more for garnish
4 teaspoons butter, divided

1 tablespoon olive oil
¾ cup Lillet (which I love using for seafood dishes) or white wine
1 tablespoon tamari sauce
zest and juice of 1 orange

Pat the scallops dry and season with salt and pepper. Place the sesame seeds in a bowl. Press the scallops into the seeds to cover all sides. Heat up 2 teaspoons of butter and olive oil in a skillet over medium heat. When the pan is hot, add the scallops and sear on each side, about 2 to 3 minutes per side; don't move them while they're cooking so a crust can form. When done, remove the scallops and add remaining butter to the pan. Add Lillet or white wine, tamari, and orange zest and juice. Simmer for 2 to 3 minutes. Pour sauce over the scallops and top with sesame seeds.

Roasted Sea Bass with Fennel Orange Salad

Serves 4

Serve the sea bass alongside the Fennel Orange Salad (page 44). What an easy, fresh dinner!

1 tablespoon olive oil
2 cloves garlic, minced
2 tablespoons fennel fronds, chopped, divided
¼ teaspoon salt, plus more for seasoning

¼ teaspoon freshly ground pepper, plus more for seasoning
4 sea bass fillets

Preheat oven to 425°F. Combine oil, garlic, 1 tablespoon of fennel fronds, and salt and pepper in a small bowl. Place sea bass fillets in a shallow baking dish. Season fillets with salt and pepper, then rub fish with the fennel mixture. Bake for 20 minutes. Remove from oven. Plate Fennel Orange Salad (page 44) and top each salad with one piece of fish. Sprinkle with remaining fennel fronds.

Wasabi-Sesame-Crusted Tuna

Serves 4

Buy sushi-grade tuna because this tuna is best served rare. If you want the best cut possible, Fish Tales in Brooklyn is one of my go-to shops. I also like the Lobster Place in Chelsea Market, Roy's Fish & Sushi, and Sea Breeze Fish Market. Serve with Wasabi Mashed Potatoes (page 99).

For the tuna
2 tablespoons mustard (I recommend Maille Original Dijon, which has some heat to it)
¼ teaspoon wasabi powder
2 tablespoons rice vinegar
2 tablespoons soy sauce
4 (6–8-ounce) pieces sushi-grade Ahi tuna
1 tablespoon sesame oil
⅓ cup of black and white sesame seeds, combined

For the sauce
¼ cup dark soy sauce
1 tablespoon mustard
1 clove garlic, minced
1 pinch wasabi powder

> **QUICK TIP**
>
> "A rich and meaty cut of tuna requires a red wine that can stand up to its hearty texture, and Joseph Swan's full-bodied Russian River Pinot Noir does the trick. This wine's flavors of bright red fruit and cinnamon complement the spicy and savory aspects of the wasabi-sesame marinade."
>
> —Henry Castro,
> Millesima NYC

In a shallow bowl, whisk together the mustard, wasabi powder, vinegar, and soy sauce. Add the tuna, pouring the sauce over it to cover. Refrigerate for 30 to 60 minutes. Heat sesame oil in a skillet over medium-high heat. Pour sesame seeds onto a plate and coat the tuna. When the oil is hot, sear tuna for 3 minutes on each side (for rare).

Mix all ingredients for the sauce together. Serve as a dipping sauce for the tuna along with sweet chili sauce, which is available at most Asian markets such as Fei Long Supermarket in Brooklyn and Bangkok Center Grocery in Manhattan's Chinatown.

Oregano-Feta-Crusted Rack of Lamb

Serves 4

There's something elegant about having rack of lamb for dinner, but no need to make dinner reservations when it's easy enough to make at home. For a lovely rack of lamb, try Staubitz Market or Ottomanelli & Sons Meat Market, an old-school Italian butcher shop. I've suggested six preparation variations, but I wholeheartedly believe in experimentation, so feel free to try different herbs and mustards for a variety of flavor combinations.

1½–2 pounds rack of lamb
salt and freshly ground pepper, to taste
¼ cup feta cheese
1 garlic clove, minced

⅓ cup bread crumbs
1 tablespoon fresh oregano, chopped
1 tablespoon mustard (I recommend Maille tap mustard with white wine)

Preheat oven to 425°F. With a sharp knife, score the top, fatty part of the lamb. Place in a roasting pan, season with salt and pepper. Combine feta cheese, garlic, bread crumbs, and oregano. Rub the lamb with mustard. Top with feta mixture. Roast for 30 minutes for medium rare, turning the rack around once after 15 minutes. Remove from oven and let sit for 10 minutes before slicing.

TRUFFLE MUSTARD HERBES DE PROVENCE RACK OF LAMB

Follow the steps up until making the feta. Rub lamb with 1 tablespoon of truffle mustard. Sprinkle with 1 tablespoon of herbes de Provence. Spread over the lamb and roast.

HONEY, SAFFRON, AND ALMONDS

Follow the steps up until making the feta. Combine ¼ cup of honey with a few strands of saffron and 1 tablespoon of crushed almonds. Spread over the lamb and roast.

HARISSA SCHWARMA

Follow the steps up until making the feta. Combine 1 teaspoon of harissa with 2 teaspoons of za'atar and 1 tablespoon of olive oil. Spread over the lamb and roast.

TRUFFLE SOY AND MISO

Follow the steps up until making the feta. Combine 2 tablespoons of truffle soy with 1 tablespoon of miso. Let sit for a few minutes. Rub onto the lamb. Sprinkle with sesame seeds.

PARSLEY AND PARMESAN

Follow the steps up until making the feta. Combine 2 tablespoons of chopped parsley with 2 tablespoons of chopped Parmesan, 1 clove of garlic, and 1 tablespoon of olive oil. You could combine everything in a small food processor. Spread over the lamb and roast.

Don't Compromise on Flavor

Strip Steak
with Kaffir-Lime Béarnaise

Serves 4

Béarnaise sauce evokes an adorable French bistro with surly waiters and flowing red wine. But, I've transformed traditional béarnaise by switching the usual tarragon and white vinegar with pungent kaffir lime and tangy rice vinegar. While a sauce made of butter and cream can seem heavy, I think it's certainly okay once in a while.

For the béarnaise
1 egg yolk
2 tablespoons butter
2 teaspoons shallots, minced
1 tablespoon rice vinegar
juice of 1 lemon
1 teaspoon Dijon mustard
¼ cup heavy cream
1 teaspoon salt
1 teaspoon freshly ground pepper
2 teaspoons kaffir lime leaves, sliced

For the steak
1 tablespoon olive oil
Salt and freshly ground pepper, to taste
4 (8-ounce) strip steaks

Make the béarnaise sauce first. Whisk the egg yolk until fluffy. Melt butter in a small saucepan over low heat. Remove from heat and whisk in the shallots, vinegar, lemon, and mustard. Beat in the egg yolk, whisking vigorously to combine all the ingredients. Place pan back on the burner over low heat. Continue to whisk until combined and somewhat thick. Add in cream, salt, and pepper and simmer for 1 to 2 minutes. Remove from heat and add lime leaves. Serve as soon as steak is done.

For the steak, heat olive oil in a skillet over medium heat. Season liberally with salt and pepper. When the pan is hot, place steak in the oil. For medium rare, cook for about 3 minutes on each side. Serve with the béarnaise sauce.

Flank Steak
with Lime and Garlic

Serves 4

Marinate the steak the night before or the morning of the day you're going to make it. Grilled skirt steak is prime for marinating because the meat absorbs the flavors well (lime, garlic, honey, mint . . . a wonderful melding of flavors). Once you're ready to grill the meat, it'll take just minutes before dinner is ready. This makes a great summertime dish to cook on the grill. You can easily double the recipe if you're having friends over.

¼ cup olive oil, plus 2 tablespoons
1 teaspoon crushed chili pepper
juice and zest of 3 limes
4 cloves garlic, minced
2 scallions, chopped

1 tablespoon honey
1 tablespoon fresh coriander, chopped
1 tablespoon fresh mint, chopped
1½ pounds flank steak

In a bowl large enough to contain the meat, combine ¼ cup of olive oil with chili pepper, lime juice and zest, garlic, scallions, honey, coriander, and mint. Add the steak. Marinate for at least 6 hours. Remove from the refrigerator 15 to 20 minutes before grilling.

Heat up the grill and grill on each side for 3 minutes for medium rare. If you aren't using a grill, you can use a grill pan over medium-high heat. If using the pan, add 2 tablespoons of olive oil. Make sure the pan is hot, then place the steak in the pan. Sear on each side for about 3 to 4 minutes for medium rare. Let rest for 5 minutes before slicing.

Grilled Mediterranean Pork Chops with Chermoula Sauce

Serves 4

Chermoula is known as a green, earthy, and fragrant sauce that's often found in North African cuisine, especially Moroccan and Tunisian. Although served often with seafood, I love it on pork chops. I love this sauce so much, I make a batch every week or so and serve it as a dip, too.

QUICK TIP

"With grilled pork, I look for a wine with a slightly toasty element. The Chacra Merlot Amor Seco 2014, a red from Argentina with an old-world inflection, showcases aromas of dark, juicy fruit, rich chocolate and coffee, and an herbaceous characteristic that pairs beautifully with pungent, aromatic spices."

—Andrew Barker,
Millesima NYC

3 cloves garlic
2 cups fresh parsley
1 cup fresh coriander
juice of 1 lemon
¼ cup olive oil, plus 1 tablespoon
¼ teaspoon cumin
¼ teaspoon ground coriander
½ teaspoon smoked paprika
1 teaspoon ancho chile pepper, crushed
4 pork chops, on the bone
salt and freshly ground pepper, to taste

Combine all ingredients except 1 tablespoon olive oil, pork chops, and salt and pepper in a food processor and blend until combined. Set sauce aside. Heat up a grill or grill pan with remaining olive oil over medium-high heat. Season the pork with salt and pepper. When the pan is hot, place the chops into the pan. Cook on each side for about 5 minutes or until just cooked through. Serve with the chermoula sauce.

Garlic-Thyme Roasted Pork Tenderloin

Serves 4

Roasted pork tenderloin is a super easy weeknight dinner because you simply rub the pork with whatever ingredients you've decided to use, and roast it in the oven while you make a side dish and set the table. Twenty-five or so minutes is just the right time for tender pork on the inside and a crisp skin on the outside.

1–1 ½ pounds pork tenderloin
salt and freshly ground pepper, to taste
1 tablespoon olive oil
2 cloves garlic, minced

2 tablespoons Dijon mustard (I recommend Maille Old Style Dijon or Original)
2 teaspoons brown sugar
1½ tablespoons fresh thyme, chopped

Preheat oven to 425°F. Season the meat with a generous amount of salt and pepper. Heat up olive oil in a large oven-proof skillet over medium-high heat. Sear the pork on all sides. Combine the remaining ingredients and spread all over the pork. Roast in the oven for 25 to 30 minutes.

JERK SPICE

Instead of the mustard, brown sugar, and thyme, combine ¼ cup pineapple juice with 1 tablespoon jerk spices, ½ teaspoon Scotch bonnet or jalapeño pepper, and 2 tablespoons bread crumbs. Spread all over the pork. Roast in the oven for 25 to 30 minutes.

SUNNY PARIS

The name of this one takes its name from the recipe's main spice blend that I use: Sunny Paris, from Penzeys Spices, which you can order online. Omit the sugar, and instead of thyme, use 1½ tablespoons Sunny Paris, which is a blend of shallots, chives, green peppercorn, dill weed, basil, tarragon, chervil, and bay leaf. Spread all over the pork. Roast in the oven for 25 to 30 minutes.

VIETNAMESE-INSPIRED

Instead of the mustard, brown sugar, and thyme, combine 1 tablespoon rice wine, 1 teaspoon fish sauce, 1 tablespoon fresh mint, and 1 tablespoon peanuts crushed in a mortar and pestle. Spread all over the pork. Roast in the oven for 25 to 30 minutes.

Dijon Chicken

Serves 4

Mustard is one of my favorite ingredients, perhaps because I love French cuisine so much. Fortunately, here in New York we have an enchanting store (with two locations) devoted to mustard: Maille. They carry mustards on tap, truffle mustard, mustard with blue cheese, mustard with arugula . . . the list goes on. If you enjoy cooking and love authentic French mustard, you'll most certainly be mesmerized by all the choices.

1 tablespoon olive oil
2 teaspoons butter
4 boneless, skinless chicken breasts
salt and freshly ground pepper,
    to taste
½ cup onion, sliced

3 tablespoons mustard (I recommend a grainy
    mustard, like the Rich Country Dijon from
    Maille)
1 cup white wine
½ cup cream
1 tablespoon fresh basil or tarragon

Heat up olive oil and butter in a skillet over medium heat. Season the chicken breasts with salt and pepper. Place chicken in the pan and cook, without moving them, for 6 to 7 minutes. Flip to the other side and cook for an additional 7 minutes. Remove the chicken. Add onions and sauté until translucent. Add the mustard and wine to the pan. Remove from heat and stir in the cream. Pour sauce over chicken and garnish with fresh basil or tarragon.

Don't Compromise on Flavor

Hummus-Crusted Chicken

Serves 4

You could make your own hummus, of course, but during the week it's easier to use already-made hummus for this easy dinner. I enjoy buying it at Pomegranate, a Kosher supermarket in Brooklyn that always has a large selection. Pomegranate is an immense store and sells a large amount of Kosher products, so you can shop for many other items there, too. You could also head to Breadberry or Gourmet Glatt Market for many other Jewish delicacies.

1 large red onion (¾ cup), sliced
3 Roma tomatoes, sliced
1 jar artichoke hearts
2 cloves garlic, minced
1 pound chicken breast or tenders

2 tablespoons olive oil
salt and freshly ground pepper, to taste
¼ cup hummus
½–1 cup white wine

Preheat oven to 450°F. Place onions, tomatoes, and artichoke hearts into a baking dish. Top with minced garlic. Place chicken on top. Rub chicken with olive oil, season with salt and pepper, then spread your favorite hummus onto the chicken; I like using roasted red pepper hummus. Pour wine into the dish, but not over the chicken. Bake for 20 minutes.

Agrodolce Chicken

Serves 4

Agrodolce, which means sweet and sour in Italian, is a fragrant and bold sauce that's wonderful on chicken along with some rice. The fresh rosemary really makes the tangy sauce stand out, so be sure to buy it fresh.

1 clove garlic, minced
¾ cup balsamic vinegar
¾ cup honey
2 scallions, chopped
1 stalk rosemary, leaves removed
1 tablespoon olive oil, plus 2 teaspoons
3 tablespoons butter
4 boneless, skinless chicken breasts
salt and freshly ground pepper, to taste
1 tablespoon Italian seasoning or other dried herb such as basil, oregano, marjoram, or thyme

For the sauce, combine garlic, vinegar, honey, scallions, and rosemary, and 1 tablespoon olive oil in a saucepan. Bring to a quick boil, then simmer for about 10 to 15 minutes. Remove from heat and stir in the butter. Heat up remaining olive oil in a skillet over medium heat. Season the chicken breasts with salt and pepper, as well as some dried Italian seasoning. Place chicken breasts in the pan and cook, without moving them, for 6 to 7 minutes. Flip to the other side and cook for an additional 7 minutes. Place chicken on a platter and top with the agrodolce sauce.

Baked Chicken
with Lime and Chickpeas

Serves 4

Garlic, capers, lime, and rosemary come together in this baked chicken dish. I've found that having an ample roasting dish makes me toss all sorts of ingredients together I might not have previously paired together. The wine steams the chicken from the bottom of the dish as it bakes, permeating the chicken and making the dish moist and flavorful.

1 cup chickpeas
2 garlic cloves, minced
2 tablespoons olive oil
2 teaspoons rosemary, chopped
8 chicken drumsticks, cleaned and patted dry
1 teaspoon salt

2 teaspoons freshly ground pepper
1 cup white wine
juice of 1 lime
2 tablespoons capers
1 lime, sliced

Preheat oven to 400°F. Combine chickpeas with garlic, olive oil, and rosemary, and place in a roasting pan. Season chicken with salt and pepper, then add the chicken to the pan, skin-side up. Drizzle white wine over the chicken and chickpeas. Next, drizzle lime juice over the chicken. Sprinkle capers on top and spread lime slices in and around the chicken. Roast in the oven for 45 minutes. Turn the chicken over and roast for 10 more minutes. If you want the skin extra crispy, turn the chicken back over and broil for 5 more minutes.

Baked Cod
with Olives and Lillet

Serves 4

There is a spice blend from Penzeys Spices that I just love called Sunny Paris. Mixing this with orange zest and bread crumbs forms a flavorful crust that doesn't overpower the delicate cod. Salty olives give the dish a bite.

QUICK TIP

"Champalou Vouvray 2015 pairs nicely with this flaky, medium-textured preparation of cod. Its honeyed, citrusy characteristics echo the orange zest and Lillet used in the dish, while its mouthwatering acidity entices you to take another bite."

—Andrew Barker,
Millesima NYC

4 (6-ounce) pieces cod
1 teaspoon salt
1 teaspoon freshly ground pepper
2 tablespoons panko bread crumbs
2 teaspoons Sunny Paris herb blend (from Penzeys Spices), or fresh parsley
zest and juice of 2 oranges, divided
1 clove garlic, minced
1 tablespoon olive oil
¼ cup green olives, chopped
1 cup Lillet

Preheat oven to 400°F. Pat the cod dry and place on a cutting board. Season with salt and pepper. Combine bread crumbs, herb blend, orange zest, garlic, and olive oil. Place cod in roasting pan. Press the panko mixture on to each piece of cod. Sprinkle chopped olives over the dish. Add Lillet and orange juice to the bottom of the pan (not over the cod). Roast in the oven for 12 to 14 minutes.

Honey-Maple Salmon

Serves 4

This oh-so-easy-to-make salmon is great on its own with rice and a side dish, on top of a watercress salad (page 49), or served over Gigli Pasta with Salmon, Zucchini, and Thai Basil (page 134). I often buy local honey and maple syrup at the Union Square Greenmarket.

2 tablespoons honey
2 tablespoons maple syrup
1 teaspoon salt

1 teaspoon freshly ground pepper
4 (6–8-ounce) salmon fillets

Preheat oven to 400°F. Combine honey and maple syrup in a bowl. Mix in salt and pepper. Place salmon in a baking dish. With a pastry brush or the back of a spoon, spread the honey-maple mixture over the salmon. Bake for about 12 minutes.

FETA- AND HERBES DE PROVENCE-CRUSTED SALMON

Preheat oven to 400°F. Sprinkle each piece of salmon with 1 teaspoon salt and 1 teaspoon pepper. Rub each piece of salmon with 2 teaspoons mustard. Combine ¼ cup feta with 1 tablespoon herbes de Provence. Coat the salmon with this mixture, then bake for about 12 minutes.

PISTACHIO-MISO-CRUSTED SALMON

Preheat oven to 400°F. Combine 1 tablespoon miso with 2 teaspoons mustard, 1 teaspoon rice vinegar, 1 teaspoon salt, and 1 teaspoon pepper. Rub salmon with this mixture, then coat with 2 tablespoons crushed pistachios. Bake for about 12 minutes.

Roasted Branzino
with Indian Spices

Serves 4

The mild flavors of branzino, a silvery-skinned Mediterranean fish, are a sweet match with aromatic Indian spices. My favorite Indian spice shops include Dual Specialty Store, Kalustyan's, and Patel Brothers.

1 (1½-pound) whole branzino, cleaned, gutted
1 tablespoon olive oil
1 teaspoon salt
1 teaspoon freshly ground pepper
2 teaspoons coriander
2 teaspoons cumin
2 teaspoons garam masala
1 teaspoon ground ginger
½ onion, sliced
1 lemon, sliced
several stalks fresh thyme
1 cup white wine

QUICK TIP

"I love Kalustyan's in Little India on Lexington Avenue. My wife Mel loves to buy Turkish spices from there."
—Scott Conant,
chef and restaurateur

Preheat oven to 400°F. Place fish in a roasting dish. Rub the fish with olive oil. Season with salt and pepper. Combine the spices and spread them on top of and inside the fish. Place onion, lemon slices, and thyme inside the fish. Add wine to the bottom of the pan. Roast for 20 to 30 minutes or until skin is crispy.

Arctic Char
with Berbere

Serves 4

I love cooking with berbere, an African spice blend consisting of cumin, garlic, coriander, ginger, basil, ajwain seeds, chili peppers, and other spices. The chili peppers give it a lot of heat, so beware if you don't like things too spicy. The berbere gives pink-fleshed arctic char a lovely scarlet hue. You could shop at Adja Khady Food Distributor or Keita West African Market, both of which sell many African spices.

4 (6-ounce) Arctic char fillets
1 teaspoon salt
1 teaspoon freshly ground pepper

1½ tablespoons berbere
1 tablespoon olive oil
2 teaspoons fresh basil, chopped

Pat the fish dry and place on a cutting board. Season with salt and pepper. Then, sprinkle berbere over the fish. Heat up olive oil in a skillet over medium heat. When the pan is hot, add the fish, berbere-side down, and cook without moving the fish for 3 to 4 minutes until a nice crust forms. Turn the fish over and cook an additional 2 to 3 minutes. Top with fresh basil.

Whole Red Snapper
with Mandarin Oranges and Oregano

Serves 4

If you want a beautiful dinner that impresses both your guests and your taste buds, try roasting a whole fish. Orange and oregano brighten up the subtle, sweet flavor of red snapper.

1 (2-pound) whole red snapper, cleaned, gutted
1 tablespoon olive oil
1 teaspoon salt
1 teaspoon freshly ground pepper

1 tablespoon herbes de Provence
2 mandarin oranges, sliced
1 tablespoon fresh oregano, plus extra for garnish
1 cup white wine

Preheat oven to 400°F. Place fish in a roasting dish and rub with olive oil. Season with salt and pepper. Sprinkle herbes de Provence on top and inside the fish. Place orange slices and oregano inside the fish. Add wine to the bottom of the pan. Roast for 20 to 30 minutes or until skin is crispy. Top with fresh oregano.

Don't Compromise on Flavor

Swordfish
with Tamarind Peanut Paste and Edamame

Serves 4

Tamarind is a popular ingredient in Indian, Southeast Asian, and Mexican cuisine. It has a somewhat bitter flavor, balanced here with peanut butter and honey. Tamarind comes in many forms; here I used a paste, which you can buy at an Indian spice shop, a Thai grocery like Bangkok Center Grocery or Inthira Thai Market, or an all-around Asian grocery such as Asia Market Corporation.

2 tablespoons tamarind paste
2 tablespoons peanut butter
1 teaspoon sesame oil
2 teaspoons soy sauce
1 tablespoon fresh lime juice
2 teaspoons honey
4 (6–8-ounce) pieces swordfish
1 tablespoon flour

1 teaspoon salt
1 teaspoon freshly ground pepper
1 tablespoon olive oil
1 cucumber, chopped
¼ cup peanuts, crushed
¼ cup edamame beans
1 tablespoon red onion, minced

Combine tamarind, peanut butter, sesame oil, soy sauce, lime juice, and honey in a bowl and set aside. Pat the swordfish dry and place on a cutting board. Combine flour with salt and pepper. Heat olive oil in a skillet over medium heat. When the oil is hot, add swordfish and cook on each side for 3 to 4 minutes. Place tamarind mixture on each plate. Place swordfish over the tamarind, then garnish with cucumber, peanuts, edamame, and red onion.

Non-Boring Side Dishes

This chapter, as the name suggests, is all about side dishes that won't leave you disappointed. Move over bland potatoes and flavorless corn, these sides will make your entire plate a feast for the senses. While many vegetables can be absolutely wonderful on their own, I like elevating the flavors even more with spices, citrus, sauces, and global ingredients. While side dishes are often literally and figuratively pushed to the side, some of these will have you rethinking what to serve with main courses.

Cumin-Broiled Eggplant

Serves 4

Eggplant is one of those vegetables that needs a little something extra to bring out its beauty, and cumin, one of my favorite spices, adds a fragrant note. Topped with crumbled blue cheese and pomegranate seeds (when in season), this broiled eggplant is pretty—and pretty tasty.

2 large eggplants, sliced lengthwise or in circles

2 cloves garlic

1 teaspoon mustard (I recommend the Honey and Modena balsamic mustard from Maille)

1 teaspoon ground cumin

½ teaspoon ground coriander

¼ cup balsamic vinegar

2 tablespoons olive oil, plus 1 tablespoon

¼ teaspoon salt

¼ teaspoon freshly ground pepper

2 tablespoons pomegranate seeds

¼ cup blue cheese, crumbled

2 tablespoons flat leaf parsley, chopped, to garnish

Slice eggplant into desired pieces. In a large bowl, combine garlic, mustard, spices, vinegar, 2 tablespoons of olive oil, and salt and pepper. Soak the eggplant in this sauce for 30 minutes. Cook the eggplant on a grill, in a grill pan, or a large skillet. If using a grill, grill eggplant on each side for 2 to 3 minutes. If using a grill pan, heat 1 tablespoon olive oil over medium heat. Add eggplant and cook for 2 to 3 minutes on each side. You may have to do this in batches. Place on a platter and garnish with pomegranate seeds, blue cheese, and parsley.

Wasabi Mashed Potatoes

Serves 4

Mashed potatoes are the perfect canvas to add some pizzazz, like pungent wasabi, aromatic and spicy jerk seasoning, or one of my favorite additions: horseradish. Jerk spices can be found at many stores, but I like buying blends at Caribbean shops like Carib Food Market and Downtown Natural Market.

1½ pounds potatoes, peeled (I recommend Yukon Gold)
½ cup whole milk
2 tablespoons sour cream
4 tablespoons butter

1 tablespoon Dijon mustard
1 teaspoon wasabi powder
1 teaspoon salt
1 teaspoon freshly ground pepper
1½ tablespoons scallions, chopped

Cut the potatoes into quarters. Place in a large saucepan and cover with water. Bring to a boil, then simmer until potatoes are soft. Drain and place in a bowl. Add remaining ingredients except for the scallions, and mash with an immersion blender or hand-held mixer. Top with chopped scallions..

CARAMELIZED ONION MASHED POTATOES WITH HORSERADISH

Omit mustard and wasabi powder. Sauté ½ cup sliced onions in butter over low heat until caramelized. Add the onion plus 1 tablespoon fresh, chopped horseradish to the potatoes before mashing.

JERK-SPICED MASHED POTATOES

Keep the mustard but omit the wasabi powder. Then, simply add 1 tablespoon jerk spice to potatoes before mashing.

Grilled Asparagus
with Lemon Zest and Sumac Crème Fraîche

Serves 4

Asparagus is one of those vegetables that's so good simply grilled with nothing added. But here I've dressed it up with lemony-crème fraîche and the unique flavor of sumac, which has a slightly tart citrus flavor.

1 pound fresh asparagus
1 teaspoon salt
1 teaspoon freshly ground pepper

zest and juice of 1 lemon, divided
2 teaspoons sumac, plus more for dusting
¼ cup crème fraîche

Preheat oven to 400°F. Parboil the asparagus by placing in boiling water for 2 minutes. Remove and place into a baking dish. Top with salt, pepper, and lemon zest. Roast in the oven for about 15 minutes. Meanwhile, mix lemon juice, sumac, and crème fraiche together. Serve this along with the asparagus. Dust with more sumac.

Brussels Sprouts with Bacon and Mustard Vinaigrette

Serves 4

Brussels sprouts and bacon are a divine pairing. Orange and mustard add some tang.

4 pieces bacon
2 pounds Brussels sprouts, halved lengthwise
1 tablespoon olive oil, plus more for drizzling
1 teaspoon salt, plus extra for seasoning

1 teaspoon freshly ground pepper, plus extra for
   seasoning
juice and zest of 1 orange
1 teaspoon Dijon mustard

First, cook the bacon. You can cook in a skillet over low-medium heat or bake at 425°F on a cookie sheet for 15 minutes until crisp. Set aside. When you're ready to make the Brussels sprouts, preheat oven to 400°F. Place sprouts on a baking sheet, drizzle with olive oil, salt, and pepper, and roast in the oven for 20 to 25 minutes. In a bowl, mix together olive oil, orange juice and zest, mustard, and salt and pepper. When done, remove from oven, toss with sauce, and add crumbled bacon.

Roasted Leeks and Zucchini
with Mint and Rice Vinegar

Serves 4

Oh, how I love leeks! I've roasted them here with zucchini as a seasonal side dish for spring with fish or lamb. I've also added this to couscous for a light, refreshing lunch. Adja Khady Food Distributor sells a wide array of couscous.

2 zucchini, halved lengthwise, then sliced into
    half-moons
2 leeks, cut into half-moon shapes
1–2 tablespoons olive oil
salt and freshly ground pepper, for seasoning

¼ cup rice vinegar
2 tablespoons mint, chopped
¼ cup feta, crumbled

Preheat oven to 350°F. Place zucchini and leeks on a cookie sheet. Drizzle with olive oil and season with salt and pepper. Roast in the oven for 10 minutes or until they start to brown. Toss with rice vinegar and top with mint and feta.

Roasted Rainbow Carrots
with Fig Balsamic and Curry Butter

Serves 4–6

The Union Square Greenmarket always has the most beautiful carrots; I usually pick up some blue and orange ones. Balsamic and curry is an unusual combination that works well with the sweetness of the carrots.

2 pounds rainbow carrots, peeled
2 tablespoons olive oil
1 teaspoon salt
1 teaspoon freshly ground pepper

2 tablespoons butter
2 teaspoons curry powder
1 tablespoon fig balsamic vinegar

Preheat oven to 375°F. Toss carrots with olive oil and salt and pepper. Place on cookie sheet. Roast in the oven for 30 to 35 minutes. Meanwhile, mash the curry powder with the butter. Remove carrots from oven and toss with the curry butter. Drizzle with balsamic vinegar.

Lemon Mustard Seed Potatoes

Serves 4

Sharp and pungent mustard seeds, often used in Indian and African dishes, give humble roasted potatoes a beautiful color and flavor.

1½ pounds whole fingerling potatoes or russet
   potatoes, quartered
1 teaspoon salt
1 teaspoon freshly ground pepper
½ cup fresh lemon juice

zest of 1 lemon
1 tablespoon mustard seeds
2 tablespoons olive oil
1 tablespoon rosemary, chopped

Preheat oven to 400°F. Toss potatoes with salt and pepper, lemon juice, lemon zest, and mustard seeds. Add olive oil to an oven-safe skillet over medium heat. Pan fry until crisp. Turn off heat, then place the pan in the oven. Roast for 30 to 35 minutes. Toss with fresh rosemary.

HOISIN ROASTED POTATOES

Omit lemon juice, zest, and mustard seeds. Toss potatoes with 1 tablespoon olive oil, salt, and pepper. After potatoes are done, toss with ¼ cup hoisin sauce, 1 tablespoon sesame seeds, and 1 tablespoon scallions.

Lentils Stewed in Red Wine
with Orange and Thyme

Serves 4

I always keep a variety of dried lentils stocked for soups, stews, and side dishes like this one that combine red wine, orange, and thyme for a truly non-boring side. Be sure not to overcook them—lentils are optimal when they have an ever-so-slight crunch.

1 tablespoon olive oil
¼ cup red onion, minced
2 cloves garlic, minced
1 cup French lentils
juice and zest of 1 large orange

1 tablespoon fresh thyme
1 teaspoon salt
1 teaspoon freshly ground pepper
2 cups red wine
1 scallion, chopped

Heat olive oil in a skillet over medium heat. Add onion and sauté until translucent. Add garlic and sauté for 1 minute. Add lentils, and stir. Add orange juice and zest, thyme, salt, and pepper. Stir for 1 minute, then add 1 cup of wine and simmer until liquid is absorbed. Add remaining wine, and possibly water or stock if needed, and continue to simmer until lentils are cooked, but still slightly al dente, about 20 minutes. Top with chopped scallions.

Non-Boring Side Dishes

Greens

Serves 4

Many meals don't feel complete unless you serve greens, and greens are certainly one of the most nutrient-rich items to eat. I love browsing the vendors in Chinatown in search of Asian greens like bok choy, gai lan, pea shoots, water spinach, Chinese broccoli, and yau choy. For broccoli rabe and spinach, I stock up at my local farmers' markets. Here are four ideas to get you inspired to eat your greens; something I often tell my daughter. You can use some of the Asian greens I mentioned for the recipes below, or stick to spinach and broccoli rabe.

For all recipes below, buy 1 pound of greens per 4 people, except for the spinach, which shrinks considerably, so go for 2 to 3 pounds. Heat up 1½ tablespoons olive oil in a skillet over medium heat and add 2 cloves garlic, minced, for all recipes. Then, sauté the greens until just wilted. Follow further directions under each.

BABY BOK CHOY WITH GINGER AND PROSCIUTTO

Add 1 ounce prosciutto, chopped, and 1 (1-inch) piece ginger, chopped, when heating up the olive oil.

SAUTÉED SPINACH WITH CHILI PEPPER AND PARMESAN

When spinach has just wilted, toss with 2 teaspoons chili pepper and ½ cup freshly grated Parmesan.

CHINESE BROCCOLI WITH OYSTER SAUCE AND GINGER

Add 1 (1-inch) piece ginger when heating up the olive oil. Add ¼ cup oyster sauce just before turning off the heat. Stir to combine.

SUGAR SNAP PEAS WITH SOY AND SUMAC

When snap peas are done, toss with 2 tablespoons soy sauce and 2 teaspoons sumac.

Acorn Squash with Saba, Sage, and a Hint of Vanilla

Serves 4

In my humble opinion, squash calls for some sweetness, so the bold and sweet saba, brown sugar, and vanilla balance the nutty flavors of the squash. Serve ½ squash per person.

2 acorn squash, halved
¼ cup saba
1 tablespoon olive oil
1 teaspoon vanilla

1 teaspoon salt
1 teaspoon freshly ground pepper
2 tablespoons brown sugar
2 teaspoons fresh sage

Preheat oven to 350°F. Place the acorn squash halves in a baking dish. Combine saba, oil, vanilla, salt, and pepper and pour into the squash, using a spoon to cover the sides. Bake for 30 minutes. Meanwhile, combine brown sugar and sage. After 30 minutes, sprinkle brown sugar/sage combination over the squash and bake for an additional 15 minutes.

Spiced Sweet Potato Fries with Truffle Ketchup

Serves 4

Adding spices with a dash of heat to roasted sweet potato fries makes for a mouthwatering treat that surpasses good ol' French fries. Dipping them in truffle ketchup makes it an even more pleasant experience. (Urbani Truffles makes a pungent truffle ketchup.)

2 pounds sweet potatoes, sliced into sticks
2 tablespoons olive oil
1 teaspoon smoked paprika
1 teaspoon cumin
1 teaspoon coriander

½ teaspoon crushed chili pepper
1 teaspoon smoked salt (I recommend Red Alder from The Meadow)
1 teaspoon freshly ground pepper

Preheat oven to 375°F. Toss the sweet potato slices with olive oil. Combine the spices, then sprinkle on the sweet potatoes. Place the sweet potatoes onto a baking sheet and bake in the oven for 30 to 35 minutes, or until desired crispness. Serve with truffle ketchup.

Pumpkin
with Truffle Cream and Crispy Shallots

Serves 4

Truffle cream from NYC-based Urbani Truffles elevates the earthy flavor of the pumpkin while crispy shallots add a lovely crunch. Top with pumpkin seeds, too, if you like. Although I've made pumpkin purée on my own, you can opt to use canned organic pumpkin purée to speed up dinner.

1 pound pumpkin, chopped
1 large onion, sliced
1½ tablespoons olive oil
1 teaspoon salt
1 teaspoon freshly ground pepper

1 tablespoon butter
2 shallots, sliced into circles
1 jar truffle cream from Urbani Truffles
2 teaspoons sage

Preheat oven to 375°F. Place pumpkin pieces and onion slices onto a baking sheet. Drizzle with olive oil, and sprinkle with salt and pepper. Roast in the oven for 45 to 50 minutes. Remove from oven and let cool for 2 to 3 minutes. Meanwhile, add butter to a small skillet over medium heat. Pan fry shallots until crispy. In a food processor, mix pumpkin and onion until puréed. Stir in truffle cream and sage. Top with crispy shallots.

Smashed White Beans
with Balsamic and Parmesan

Serves 4

I had a dish like this once in Rome. I loved the simplicity of the white beans, garlic, balsamic, and Parmesan so much that I recreated it here.

1½ cups dry white beans soaked in water overnight, or 2 cans
1 tablespoon olive oil
3 cloves garlic, chopped
½ cup white wine

2 tablespoons balsamic vinegar, plus more for drizzling
½ cup freshly grated or shaved Parmesan
1 tablespoon fresh sage, chopped

If you're using dry beans that have been soaking overnight, drain them first, then place them in a pot with cold water, and boil until soft. Drain again. If you're using canned, simply rinse and drain. Heat olive oil in a skillet over medium heat. Add garlic and cook until crisp. Add the beans and stir. Add wine and continue to stir. Add balsamic vinegar; stir, then remove from stove. Sprinkle with Parmesan. Drizzle with more balsamic, if you like, and add some fresh sage.

Compelling Carbs

Pasta, Rice, and Other Grains

When I first moved to New York I lived several blocks from two disparate stores I frequented on a very regular basis: Hong Kong Supermarket and Di Palo's Fine Foods, both of which inspired me to cook at home even though there were hundreds of restaurants nearby. Di Palo's is one of those stores that transports you to Italy; it's full of pasta, bread, cheese, and cured meats—and it's always bustling. Di Palo's is warm and welcoming, with siblings Sal, Lou, and Marie eager to answer any questions or offer you a taste of cheese or cured meat. Be prepared to take a number and wait 10 to 15 minutes (especially on the weekends). But trust me, it's worth it. Hong Kong Supermarket is also bustling, but on a larger scale. Shoppers from blocks and boroughs away stock up on Asian greens (what an amazing selection!), meat, poultry, fish, and noodles. I come here for udon, miso, Asian condiments, ginger, and obscure greens, and their coconut bread (which makes a wonderful French toast).

While there are many other places to find pasta and rice, you'll undoubtedly find countless ingredients you'll want to take home from both Di Palo's and Hong Kong Supermarket, which you'll find in the recipes that follow. And while I recommend certain types, please do experiment with your own discoveries.

Chinese Five-Spice Pumpkin Risotto with Blue Cheese

Serves 4

The combination of pumpkin, sage, and Chinese five-spice is one I experimented with on a blustery fall day. Chinese five-spice can vary from store to store but is generally a blend of Szechuan pepper, star anise, cloves, cinnamon, and fennel seeds. You can find it at Asian markets and also at charming shops like Sullivan Street Tea & Spice Company or Two for the Pot.

3 cups fresh pumpkin, peeled, cubed
1 tablespoon Chinese five-spice
1 tablespoon butter
4 shallots, chopped
5 cups chicken stock
2 cups Arborio rice

¼ cup white wine
½ teaspoon saffron
1 tablespoon fresh sage, chopped
¼ cup semi-firm crumbled blue cheese
sea salt and freshly ground black pepper, to taste

Place pumpkin in tin foil and sprinkle with Chinese five-spice. Close the foil and bake at 350°F for 30 minutes. Meanwhile, melt butter over low heat and sauté shallots. In a separate pan, bring the stock to a boil, then reduce heat to simmer. Once pumpkin is cooked, purée it in a food processor or immersion blender and set aside. Add the Arborio rice to the shallots and cook for about 2 to 3 minutes over medium heat, stirring frequently. Add white wine and saffron and cook, stirring constantly until all the liquid has been absorbed. Add the pumpkin and 1 cup of stock, stirring constantly. After that is absorbed, add the rest of the stock, about ½ cup at a time. Stir constantly until absorbed and until the rice is cooked, about 15 to 20 minutes for al dente. If you run out of stock, add more white wine or some warm water. The risotto should be thick and creamy, and only slightly runny. When done, remove from heat and add the sage, cheese, and salt and pepper to taste.

QUICK TIP

Arborio rice is the most popular grain for risotto, but you can also use short grain rice like Apollo, Baldo, Carnaroli, and Vialone Nano, all of which are sold at Eataly, Kalustyan's and Il Buco Alimentari. These types of rice have a high starch content that is released during the cooking process, allowing it to be more absorbent.

QUICK TIP

"Make sure the stock is hot. If the stock is cold, it will shock the rice and prevent it from releasing its starch. I also like to use hot water about ⅔ of the way through. If you are adding butter, olive oil, or cheese to finish it, the end result will be very rich with all that starch. The water will cut it so the palate is not overwhelmed."

—Chef Alex Pilas, Eataly

WINE SUGGESTIONS

"The sweetness of the pumpkin and the Chinese five-spice in this risotto take center stage. A fruity New World Sauvignon Blanc is a fine choice. Selections from California will be less astringent or searing in its acidity and the most classic choice to mingle with the blue cheese. For an adventure, go for a medium-bodied Gewürztraminer from Germany or Canada; its mélange of soft floral fruitiness with exotic notes will hit all the right counterpoints with this dish." —Elizabeth Patrick, Astor Wines

Ginger and Garlic Shrimp
with Rice

Serves 4

Make your favorite rice to serve with this Asian shrimp dish. Chinese cooking wine is available at most Asian markets, including Fei Long and Hong Kong Supermarkets. My friend, who is Asian, told me to add a capful of it at the end of cooking. I added it sooner here so that the peas could simmer in it, but either way, the wine adds an authentic Asian flavor that's hard to recreate unless you use this wine.

1 cup dry rice, cooked
2 tablespoons soy sauce
1 teaspoon sesame oil
¼ teaspoon jalapeño pepper, minced
1 teaspoon Thai basil, chopped
1 tablespoon olive oil
3 garlic cloves, minced
1 (1-inch) piece ginger, minced

1 red pepper, sliced
½ cup Chinese cooking wine or regular white wine
½ cup frozen peas
16–20 shrimp
2 scallions, chopped
2 teaspoons sesame seeds

First, prepare your favorite rice. In a small bowl, combine soy sauce, sesame oil, jalapeño pepper, and Thai basil. Set aside. In a skillet or wok, heat up olive oil over medium heat. Sauté garlic and ginger for 1 to 2 minutes. Add red pepper, and stir. Add in Chinese cooking wine, then add peas and simmer until they're cooked. Add shrimp and cook, turning shrimp over when they turn pink. When they're almost done, add the sauce. Lower heat and simmer for just a few more minutes. Serve over rice, then top with scallions and sesame seeds.

Spring Risotto

Serves 4

I absolutely love springtime in New York City; walking through Shakespeare Garden in Central Park, over the Brooklyn Bridge, or through the Union Square Greenmarket to peek at all the spring produce. Spring is the time for a few of my favorite ingredients: morel mushrooms, ramps, fiddlehead ferns, peas, and radicchio, to name a few. The bitter radicchio, earthy morels, and tangy Parmesan come together to form this dreamy risotto.

1 cup fresh morels
2 tablespoons butter
1 cup ramps, chopped into bite-sized pieces
2 cups fresh peas
1 cup radicchio, sliced
5 cups vegetable or chicken broth
¼ cup extra-virgin olive oil
1 large onion, chopped
2 cups Arborio rice or other grain*

2 pinches salt, divided (I recommend a smoked sea salt from The Meadow called Halen Mon Gold. This salt won an award, but more importantly, it adds an oaky flavor to this dish, which works well with the morels)
1 cup of dry white wine
1 cup grated Parmesan
fresh oregano, to garnish

Bring 3 cups of water to a boil and add morels, then simmer for about 5 minutes. Remove mushrooms and save mushroom broth. When the mushrooms are cool, slice them into circles. Heat the butter over low-medium heat in a sauté pan, until it's foaming. Add the ramps and sauté for about 2 minutes. Add the peas, radicchio, and sliced mushrooms, and sauté for an additional 2 minutes. Set aside.

Add chicken or vegetable broth to a separate pot and bring to a boil over high heat. Then, lower heat and simmer. In a medium pot (I use the 3½-quart Le Creuset Oval Dutch oven), heat olive oil, then add onion and 1 pinch of salt. Sauté for about 10 minutes, stirring frequently. Add in ¼ cup of the simmering broth, then lower the heat. Cook for another 5 to 10 minutes, until broth evaporates. Increase heat to about medium and add rice. Cook for 3 minutes, stirring constantly, to coat the rice until it's glistening. Add 1 pinch of salt, then some wine, and stir. Ladle in some broth and continue to stir, alternating between broth and wine. Add the morels and 1 cup of the mushroom broth, and keep stirring. Continue stirring and adding in wine and broth, until the mushroom broth is absorbed. When it's just about done (the rice should be al dente), add in the mixture of ramps and radicchio; stir. Remove from heat and stir in grated cheese to taste, about 1 cup. Top with fresh oregano.

*See tip box on page 114.

Compelling Carbs

Asian Risotto

Serves 4

While risotto is an Italian dish, there's no reason you can't use Arborio rice as a canvas for other flavors, like I did here by adding garlic, ginger, sake, and Thai basil.

1 tablespoon olive oil
2 teaspoons sesame oil
1 medium yellow onion, diced
3 cloves garlic, minced
1 tablespoon ginger, grated
1½ cups Arborio rice
1 red pepper, diced
2 ounces shiitake mushrooms, diced
4 cups chicken or vegetable stock

1 cup sake
½ cup asparagus, small chopped
2 tablespoons unsalted butter
½ cup freshly grated Parmesan cheese
1 tablespoon Thai basil, chopped, plus extra for garnish
¼ teaspoon salt
¼ teaspoon freshly ground pepper

In a large sauté pan, heat olive oil and sesame oil over medium heat. Add the onion and sauté until translucent, about 1 to 2 minutes. Add the garlic and ginger and continue to stir. Add rice and stir for about 2 minutes, until rice is covered with oil. Add pepper and mushrooms. Continue to stir for another minute. Start adding in stock and sake, alternating each while stirring. Continue stirring and adding liquid for about 10 minutes. Add asparagus and cook, while stirring, for 10 minutes until rice is al dente. Turn off the heat once the rice is cooked. Fold in butter, Parmesan, and Thai basil. Top with additional Thai basil and season with salt and pepper.

Gnocchi
with Tomatoes, Pancetta, and Arugula

Serves 4

New York is full of places to buy fresh pasta, from Borgatti's Ravioli & Egg Noodles to D. Coluccio & Sons to Russo's Mozzarella & Pasta, all of which I like to visit. But I must say, Eataly truly has an outstanding choice. All of their pasta is made with local eggs and is handmade every day in more shapes than you could possibly imagine. For this recipe, try their fresh pillowy gnocchi. Eataly also offers classes where you can learn how to make your own pasta at home!

QUICK TIP

Pancetta is an Italian-cured bacon. You can pick up pancetta at so many places, but I head to Di Palo's, Esposito & Sons Pork Store, and Stinky Bklyn. Have them cut a thick piece so you can chop it into thick chunks.

1 pound gnocchi
2 ounces pancetta, cubed
3 cloves garlic, chopped
2 large tomatoes, chopped
½ teaspoon sugar
¼ teaspoon crushed red pepper
2 teaspoons saba
1 pinch sea salt
1 bunch arugula, chopped
freshly grated Parmesan, to taste

Begin with boiling water for the gnocchi. Meanwhile, sauté pancetta in a large skillet over medium heat. Stir occasionally until it browns, about 5 to 7 minutes, until crisp. Add garlic and cook, stirring for 1 minute. Add tomatoes, sugar, and crushed red pepper, and stir until the tomatoes are almost completely broken down, about 5 minutes. Stir in saba and salt. Remove from the heat.

Cook gnocchi in the boiling water according to package directions. Place arugula in a colander and drain the gnocchi over it, which will wilt the arugula slightly. Add the gnocchi and arugula to the sauce in the pan; toss to combine. Serve with grated Parmesan, to taste.

Tagliatelle Pasta
with Lemon, Olives, and Prosciutto

Serves 4

If your palate likes salty/citrusy dishes, then you'll enjoy this pasta dish. There are so many wonderful places to buy prosciutto, but my favorite is Di Palo's where co-owner Sal often offers samples of something new he's brought over from Italy. Di Palo's is so popular that if you're not in the mood to wait in line, go at an off time, like 9 a.m. during a blizzard; that's one of the only times I've never had to wait.

QUICK TIP

For olives, I've found the best selection at Titan Foods in Astoria, Ninth Street International Foods in Hell's Kitchen, or Sahadi's in Brooklyn Heights.

QUICK TIP

For fresh pasta, stop by Borgatti's Ravioli & Egg Noodles, Eataly, Il Buco Alimentari, or Piemonte Ravioli.

¼ cup fresh-squeezed lemon juice
sea salt, to taste
½ cup extra-virgin olive oil
1 pinch crushed red pepper
8 ounces prosciutto, cut into small strips
½ cup green olives, diced
fresh thyme, to taste
zest of 2 lemons
freshly ground pepper, to taste
1 pound fresh tagliatelle pasta

In a small bowl, mix lemon juice with salt, olive oil, and crushed red pepper. Set aside. In a separate bowl, combine prosciutto, olives, thyme, and lemon zest. Add salt and pepper, to taste, and set aside. Cook pasta according to al dente directions. Drain water and add pasta to the bowl of prosciutto/olives. Top with lemon mixture and serve immediately.

Asian Spaghetti
with Shrimp

Serves 4

How much do I love Thai basil? Oh, so much, and I think you'll love its purple stems and faint taste of licorice. You'll find most of what you need for this recipe at Bangkok Center Grocery, a tiny store jam-packed with Thai ingredients.

1 tablespoon peanut oil
2 tablespoons fresh ginger, peeled, minced
2 cloves garlic, minced
1 cup shiitake or button mushrooms
1 red pepper, chopped
20 shrimp, tails intact
3 tablespoons sesame oil
2 tablespoons soy sauce
2 teaspoons sriracha
1½ teaspoons salt
1 pound spaghetti
1 tablespoon Thai basil, chopped
4 scallions, thinly sliced
¼ cup peanuts, crushed in a mortar and pestle
1 tablespoon sesame seeds

WINE SUGGESTIONS

"A mildly tart and fruity (bordering off-dry) wine is best for this umami-laden pasta dish. Try to find one with lower alcohol to complement the heat in this dish, perhaps a densely-fruited rosé with fruit-forward accessibility from Italy or southern France. Rounded red wines from Italy, like dolcetto, can work, too. An Amontillado or Oloroso sherry also suit the complexity of this dish."
—Elizabeth Patrick,
Astor Wines

Heat peanut oil in small skillet over medium heat. Add ginger and garlic; sauté 1 minute. Add mushrooms and pepper, and sauté for 3 to 4 minutes. Add shrimp and sauté until cooked, about 3 to 4 minutes. Transfer to a large bowl. Add sesame oil, soy sauce, sriracha, and salt, and whisk to blend. Cook spaghetti according to al dente directions. Use half a cup of pasta water and add it to the sesame oil mixture. When pasta is ready, drain and toss everything together, mixing in with Thai basil. Garnish with scallions, peanuts, and sesame seeds.

Compelling Carbs

Fusilli
with Spinach and Garlic-Parsley Butter

Serves 4

Crushing spices and fresh herbs with butter is an easy way to transform a dish. Once you smash butter with parsley, zest, and garlic in a mortar and pestle, you might find yourself adding other herbs and ingredients in the future. Buy fusilli—or another quirky medium-shaped pasta—at Piemonte Ravioli, Russo's Mozzarella & Pasta, or Eataly, where you can ogle fresh pasta being made behind the counter.

½ cup fresh parsley, chopped
2 teaspoons lemon zest
1 garlic clove
1 stick butter at room temperature
½ teaspoon sea salt
½ teaspoon freshly ground pepper
1 pound fresh fusilli
4 cups baby spinach
freshly ground Parmesan, to taste

> **QUICK TIP**
>
> I believe in using a high-quality butter when I get the chance to buy some. A local or European brand is often creamier and more flavorful than general supermarket brands. Try Eataly, which sells lots of European butter, or a cheese shop like Murray's Cheese that sells artisanal cheese; both stores sell butter from local farms and dairies.

Combine parsley, lemon zest, and garlic in a mortar and pestle or food processor. Add butter and process until well-blended. Season with salt and pepper. Cover in a bowl and refrigerate. This can be made ahead of time, but bring to room temperature before using.

Cook pasta according to package directions. When pasta is al dente, toss the spinach into the water until it wilts. Drain and combine with desired amount of parsley butter in a serving bowl. Season with salt and pepper, to taste, and Parmesan, if desired.

Vietnamese Shrimp Noodles

Serves 4

I love going out for Vietnamese noodles so much that I learned how to make them at home. The key is a good fish sauce and rice noodles. You can buy these at any Asian market, but I love perusing all the options at Fei Long and Hong Kong Supermarkets.

1 tablespoon fish sauce
juice of 3 limes
2 tablespoons sugar
3 cloves garlic, minced
1 jalapeño pepper, minced
1½ tablespoons olive oil
20 shrimp, tails intact

10 ounces rice noodles
1½ cups carrots, grated
1 red pepper, chopped
1 cucumber, chopped
1½ cups fresh mint, chopped
¼ cup peanuts, crushed

Combine fish sauce, lime juice, sugar, garlic, and jalapeño in a bowl. Set aside, but toss ¼ cup of this sauce with the uncooked shrimp. Meanwhile, heat olive oil in a large skillet over medium heat. Add the shrimp and cook until pink, about 2 minutes per side. Remove from pan. In a medium-sized saucepan, bring water to a boil. When water has boiled, add the rice noodles according to package directions. They usually take just a few minutes to cook. Add the drained noodles to a bowl. Toss in the cooked shrimp, carrots, pepper, cucumber, and 1 cup mint. Add the remaining sauce and toss to combine. Top with remaining mint and crushed peanuts.

Orecchiette
with Peas, Mint, and Lemon

Serves 4

When spring rolls around, I love using fresh mint in drinks, salads, and dinners. You can find it everywhere, but I like getting a bunch from the Union Square Greenmarket. For this dish, I use La Tur cheese: a creamy blend of cow's, goat's, and sheep's milk, from Murray's Cheese. But I also love stopping into The French Cheese Board in SoHo for a wheel of their buttery triple cream cheese.

1 pound orecchiette
½ pound fresh peas
½ cup olive oil
zest of ½ lemon
1 tablespoon fresh mint, chopped,
    plus extra to garnish

3 ounces fresh goat cheese or other soft cheese
½ teaspoon sea salt
½ teaspoon freshly ground pepper

Place pasta in boiling water. After 6 minutes, add in peas and cook for 3 more minutes, until pasta is al dente. Drain pasta and peas, reserving ½ cup pasta water. In a large bowl, combine olive oil, lemon zest, and mint. Crumble the cheese and add to the bowl. Add the pasta, peas, and ½ cup pasta water to the bowl with the goat cheese. Toss to combine. Season with salt and pepper, and garnish with fresh mint.

Whole Wheat Spaghetti
with Walnut-Arugula Pesto

Serves 4

Whole wheat, walnuts, and pesto is an earthy, crunchy combination I just love along with a glass of white wine and a slice of Epi East Side baguette from Maison Kayser or Miche bread from Bien Cuit.

1 pound whole wheat spaghetti
½ cup extra-virgin olive oil plus 1 tablespoon
¾ cup walnuts
2 cloves garlic, crushed
zest of 1 whole lemon
3 tablespoons fresh lemon juice
3 cups baby arugula leaves, stems removed
¼ teaspoon crushed red pepper
1 Peppadew pepper
½ cup fresh Parmesan
1 teaspoon Red Alder salt
½ teaspoon freshly ground pepper (I recommend
    tellicherry pepper from The Meadow)
½ pound fresh mozzarella, shredded
4–5 basil leaves, sliced into slivers

QUICK TIP

Tasting just-made mozzarella is one of life's small joys. You can watch it being made—and taste a bite—at Eataly and Casa Della Mozzarella.

QUICK TIP

A traditional pesto is made with pine nuts, which you can use here, too. But I like the earthiness of the walnuts with the whole wheat pasta.

Cook spaghetti until al dente, then strain and set aside. Meanwhile, add 1 tablespoon olive oil to a skillet over medium heat. Add walnuts and cook for about 3 minutes, stirring. Remove from pan and to a food processor, and combine with garlic, lemon zest and juice, arugula, crushed red pepper, Peppadew pepper, Parmesan, salt, and pepper. Slowly add in the remaining olive oil. Combine with pasta and top with mozzarella and basil.

Butternut Squash Ravioli with Japanese Seven-Spice

Serves 4

As cliché as it is, autumn is my favorite season in New York City, and it's when I love cooking with squash, pumpkin, and sage. For this dish, you don't have to stick to the butternut squash ravioli—use whatever "pasta "ripiena" (a.k.a. filled pasta) you like. Places to find filled pasta are Eataly and Borgatti's Ravioli & Egg Noodles, which sell a porcini ravioli that would also work well with this dish.

1 butternut squash, peeled, deseeded, cut into
   ½-inch cubes
1 onion, chopped
½ cup plus 2 tablespoons extra-virgin olive oil
2 teaspoons brown sugar
2 teaspoons Japanese seven-spice
Red Alder salt, to taste

freshly ground black pepper, to taste
1 pound filled pasta such as ravioli or tortellini
10–12 large sage leaves
¼ cup chicken stock
¼ cup white wine
Parmesan, to taste

Preheat oven to 400°F. Toss the squash with the onion and 2 tablespoons olive oil. Then, sprinkle with brown sugar, Japanese seven-spice, and salt and pepper. Place on baking sheet and roast for 30 to 40 minutes until caramelized. Cook the pasta until al dente, then strain and set aside. Heat ½ cup olive oil in a large skillet over medium heat. Once the oil is hot, fry the sage leaves until the oil stops sizzling and the edges are crisp. Drain on a paper towel. Add the squash mixture and tortellini to a skillet. Add in the stock and wine. Bring to a boil and season with salt and pepper. Remove from pan and toss with Parmesan. Garnish with fried sage and sprinkle with Japanese seven-spice.

QUICK TIP

Salt at The Meadow will make your head spin! They carry so many delicious options, but for this dish, I used Red Alder smoked salt, which imparts a smoky flavor to the squash.

WINE SUGGESTIONS

"A fuller bodied, spicy white wine is ideal. The sweetness in this rich pasta calls for an off-dry offering, as well. Pinot Gris from Alsace or a fruit-forward style from Oregon is best. For a contrast, try a Piedmontese white like Roero or a Friuli Malvasia to provide a tangy counterpoint to the sweet/savory pumpkin in this dish."

—Elizabeth Patrick, Astor Wines

Gigli Pasta
with Salmon, Zucchini, and Thai Basil

Serves 4

Thai basil is a fragrant, sweet herb, popular in many Asian cuisines from Thai to Vietnamese. Just a small amount adds spice and pungency to this otherwise delicate dish.

1 pound gigli or other small-shaped pasta
2 tablespoons extra-virgin olive oil
2 shallots, minced
2 teaspoons chopped chili pepper
1 cup zucchini, sliced into sticks
½ cup sake
1 cup lemon juice
honey-maple salmon (see recipe on page 87)
8 Thai basil leaves, sliced into slivers

Preheat oven to 350°F. Boil water and cook pasta until it's al dente. Strain and reserve some of the pasta water. Meanwhile, in a sauté pan, heat olive oil. Sauté shallots and chili pepper for 2 to 3 minutes. Add zucchini and continue to sauté for 2 to 3 more minutes. Add sake and lemon juice. Simmer for 5 minutes. Meanwhile, make honey-maple salmon (page 87) and chop the salmon into pieces. Toss pasta with the zucchini mixture and top with salmon and slivers of Thai basil.

QUICK TIP

While large supermarkets have great selections, I enjoy buying fish from local stores that specialize in seafood, because it can be fun to talk to the fishmongers, and because they often have the freshest catch. Two places I recommend are Sea Breeze in Bensonhurst and Wild Edibles in Midtown Manhattan.

QUICK TIP

You can find handmade gigli at the Arthur Avenue Retail Market in the Bronx. You can also swap in another small-shaped pasta that you like.

Baked Shrimp
with Orzo and Ouzo

Serves 4

The wonders of Titan Foods in Astoria are many, but the main draw, in my opinion, is the variety of feta cheese. You won't find that bland, crumbled, dare I say absolutely tasteless, supermarket feta at Titan. Sample a few and take home your favorite for this dish, or to eat with flatbread and dips.

1 cup orzo
juice of 1 lemon
½ cup extra-virgin olive oil, plus extra for drizzling
½ cup ouzo
2 teaspoons sea salt, plus more to garnish
1 teaspoon freshly ground black pepper, plus more to garnish

16 shrimp, peeled, deveined
2 teaspoons crushed coriander
2 teaspoons crushed cumin
½ cup minced scallions
½ cup fresh oregano, chopped
1 cucumber, peeled (if desired), deseeded, diced
¼ cup red onion, small diced
½ pound feta cheese, large diced

Preheat the oven to 400°F. Cook orzo according to package directions, until al dente. Whisk together the lemon juice, olive oil, ouzo, 2 teaspoons salt, and 1 teaspoon pepper. Pour over the hot orzo and stir well.

Place the shrimp on a cookie sheet, then rub with the coriander and cumin. Drizzle with olive oil, and sprinkle with salt and pepper. Toss to combine and spread out in a single layer. Roast for 5 to 6 minutes, until the shrimp are cooked through; be mindful not to overcook.

Add the shrimp to the orzo and then add the scallions, oregano, cucumber, and onion, with salt and pepper to taste. Toss well. Add the feta and stir. Set aside at room temperature for 1 hour to allow the flavors to blend. You can also refrigerate overnight and return to room temperature before serving.

Lobster Ravioli
with Orange-Tarragon Butter

Serves 4

A flavorful ravioli like lobster doesn't need much sauce to enhance it. Simply crushing orange and tarragon into butter makes a flavorful, acidic, yet sweet sauce.

QUICK TIP

I occasionally shop at Piemonte Ravioli in NYC's waning Little Italy for their lobster ravioli. This place has been around for over one hundred years, and they take their pasta *very* seriously. You could also make this with their goat cheese, sun-dried tomato, or artichoke ravioli, or hop down the street to Di Palo's for other fresh pasta options.

1 pound lobster ravioli
½ stick fresh butter
2 teaspoons fresh orange juice
zest of 1 orange
2 tablespoons fresh tarragon, plus more to garnish
1 teaspoon salt (I recommend lemon flake sea salt from The Meadow)
1 teaspoon black and white sesame seeds
½ teaspoon white pepper

Bring a pot of water to a boil. Meanwhile, in a mortar and pestle or bowl, crush the butter with orange juice, orange zest, tarragon, salt, and sesame seeds until combined. Refrigerate until ready to use. This can be made ahead of time.

Add ravioli to the boiling water and cook for 6 minutes. When ravioli are al dente, drain them and place on a plate or in a bowl. Add a tablespoon of the orange-tarragon butter onto the hot ravioli. Garnish with extra tarragon and white pepper.

Relax on the Weekend

Feasts

Weekends in NYC are for running jaunts around the city interspersed with some relaxation, if that's even possible in a city where there's so much to do and see. One weekend day is usually spent out and about with my daughter at bookstores (McNally Jackson, Books of Wonder), museums (The Met, The Museum of Natural History, MoMA), weekend markets (of which there are several), and, once in a while, a movie. Another weekend day is spent at home. This is when I can linger over bagels and lox or cook a more complex and time-consuming meal, like tagine or paella, both of which require more effort than weekday dinners.

Paella

Serves 4–6

Paella is a very versatile dish. You can add all different kinds of meat and seafood, but I always make sure my paella has two authentic ingredients: chorizo and smoked paprika, both of which impart heat and a smoky flavor to this swoon-worthy, dinner party dish.

1 teaspoon saffron
½ cup Spanish white wine, plus 3 cups, divided
2 tablespoons olive oil
1 small shallot, sliced
1 medium white or yellow onion
4 ounces spicy chorizo
4 cloves garlic
2 cups Arborio rice
3 tomatoes (I recommend Roma)

1 teaspoon smoked paprika
1 small, dried ancho chile pepper (1 teaspoon), crushed
1 teaspoon salt
1–2 teaspoons freshly ground pepper
1 pound shrimp
½ pound mussels
1 pound cockles
2 tablespoons Italian flat leaf parsley, chopped

Soak the saffron in ½ cup wine. Then, in a large skillet (I use the gorgeous paella pan from Mauviel shown in the photo) add the olive oil, shallot, and onion and cook over medium heat. Sauté the onion until translucent. Add the chorizo. Sauté for 1 to 2 minutes, while stirring so the onion doesn't burn. Add the garlic and stir. Then, add the rice and stir until rice is coated. Pour in the saffron/wine mixture. Add tomatoes, spices, salt, and pepper. Add 1 cup of wine and stir, and continue to add the remaining wine if the rice starts to dry. Once rice is almost cooked, add the shrimp and cover with the rice. Cook for 5 more minutes, adding more wine or water if needed. Add mussels, then cockles. Once the shellfish open up, the paella is ready to be served. Garnish with parsley.

QUICK TIP

For Spanish ingredients, I love going to Despa-ña in SoHo. They sell ingredients specifically for paella, including rice, chorizo, spices, and even a whole gift basket for paella lovers.

WINE SUGGESTIONS

"Paella is like Thanksgiving—it pairs well with whatever you're in the mood to drink! Between the spice, smoke, herbs, and brine, there are flavors that play nicely with just about any category of wine. Fino and Amontillado sherries are inspired pairings for the constellation of flavors in this paella, offering more density, structure, alcohol, and complex flavors of yeast and umami than the average table wine."
—Ariana Rolich, Chambers Street Wines

Chicken Tagine

Serves 4–6

I love how my kitchen smells while a tagine is roasting in the oven. All those exotic spices swirling around are so intoxicating that I make this dish at least once a month. Get yourself an actual tagine dish, for optimal cooking, like the one pictured from Emile Henry, or use a Dutch oven or other large pan with a cover. Part of the fun of this dish is mixing the spices; you don't have to adhere to what I mixed together—feel free to improvise!

2 tablespoons sweet paprika
1 teaspoon garlic powder
2 teaspoons cinnamon
2 tablespoons ground coriander
1 teaspoon cardamom
2 teaspoons allspice
1 teaspoon cumin seeds
2 tablespoons olive oil

3 pounds chicken pieces (breast and/or thigh)
coarse salt and freshly ground pepper, to taste
1 large red or yellow onion, sliced into circles
2 medium-sized potatoes, sliced into circles
3 tomatoes, chopped (I recommend Roma)
¾ cup olives (I recommend green Castelvetrano)
zest of 1 lemon
1 cup of water

Preheat oven to 325°F. In a small bowl, combine spices and set aside. Season chicken with salt and pepper. Add olive oil to a large skillet over medium heat. Brown chicken for about 5 minutes on each side. Remove from pan and set aside. In a tagine, arrange onion slices so they cover the bottom of the dish. Add potato slices in the same manner. Arrange chicken on top of the potatoes. Toss tomatoes and olives around the dish. Sprinkle with lemon zest and spice mixture. Add water to the bottom of the tagine. Cook in the oven for about 75 minutes. After 45 minutes, check to see if the dish needs more water.

WINE SUGGESTIONS

"This Moroccan classic offers an array of aromatic flavors shared by Lieu Dit Sauvignon Blanc 2015, a popular Sauvignon Blanc, which showcases citrus and stone fruit. The wine's tart, refreshing finish cuts through the tagine's layered complexity."
—Henry Castro, Millesima NYC

QUICK TIP

"La Boîte is one of my favorite specialty stores in New York. Lior is a master of blending spices. His range of spices is like no other and is so vast, from all corners of the world. It's hard not to be inspired by the colors and aromas in his store—it's something really magical."
—Chef Eric Ripert, Le Bernardin

Fettucine
with Szechuan Peppercorn Short Rib Ragout

Serves 4–8

Swaths of freshly-made fettucine are ripe for a hearty sauce. And nothing beats freshly-made pasta so try and opt for that when you can: Russo's, Eataly, Borgatti's Ravioli & Egg Noodles, D. Coluccio & Sons . . . there are many options for fresh pasta of all kinds. This is a dish best made when you have a block of time, or you can make the short ribs on the weekend, then serve this during the week.

2 tablespoons extra-virgin olive oil
2 ounces pancetta
4 pounds short ribs
1 teaspoon kosher salt
1 teaspoon freshly ground pepper
2 shallots, chopped
2 cloves garlic, minced
2 tablespoons Szechuan peppercorns, crushed in a mortar and pestle
1 bay leaf
2 teaspoons fresh rosemary, chopped

2 teaspoons fresh thyme, chopped
2 teaspoons fresh parsley, chopped
1 tablespoon fresh ginger, minced
½ cup brown sugar
½ cup pineapple juice
2 tablespoons tomato paste
1 (14-ounce) can crushed tomatoes
¼ cup dark soy sauce
1 cup red wine
1 cup beef broth
2 pounds fettucine

You can make the ragout ahead of time. In fact, I suggest it so that the flavors can meld together. Preheat oven to 325°F. Heat olive oil in a cast-iron pot or a Dutch oven (I use a 6-quart Le Creuset Dutch oven) over medium-high heat. Add pancetta and cook for 4 to 5 minutes, until crisp. Season the short ribs with salt and pepper, then braise in olive oil for a few minutes on each side until browned. Remove from pan. Add shallots and garlic and sauté until the shallots are translucent. Add peppercorns, bay leaf, rosemary, thyme, parsley, ginger, brown sugar, pineapple juice, tomato paste, crushed tomatoes, soy sauce, wine, and beef broth. Simmer for about 15 minutes. Place short ribs back into the pot, cover, and place in oven for 3 hours. Once done, remove from oven, and remove the bones. When you're ready to serve, place the pot over medium heat and simmer for about 10 to 15 minutes. Meanwhile, cook the fettucine until al dente, about 3 minutes. Combine the pasta with ragout and serve.

QUICK TIP

"When buying short ribs, look for a nice marbled piece of meat with a fair amount of fat left on. The fat is what makes short ribs so rich and delicious, and will break down during cooking. Don't be afraid of flavor. A good butcher will cut meat to your requested size, so make sure you ask your butcher to cut them to the size you desire." —Fleishers Craft Butchery

Spaghetti Bolognese

Serves 6

Here is another wonderful pasta dish to make on the weekend. This makes enough that you might have leftovers for an easy weekday meal. I like to use a combination of beef, pork, and veal. You can mix it up however you like, though I'd definitely suggest using at least two types of ground meat for a richer flavor.

1 tablespoon olive oil
1 medium onion, chopped
3 cloves garlic
1 cup carrots, chopped
1 cup celery chopped
½ pound ground beef
½ pound ground pork
½ pound ground veal
¼–½ teaspoon salt
¼–½ teaspoon freshly ground pepper

1 (28-ounce) can crushed tomatoes
1 tablespoon fresh thyme
1 tablespoon fresh oregano
1 tablespoon fresh basil
1 cup red wine
½ teaspoon nutmeg
¾ cup cream
fresh Parmesan, for serving
1 pound spaghetti

Heat olive oil in a large skillet over medium heat. Sauté onion until translucent, about 1 to 2 minutes. Add garlic and stir. Add carrots and celery; cook for 3 to 4 minutes. Add beef, pork, and veal, breaking up the meat while stirring. Add salt and pepper. Once the meat is brown, about 5 to 6 more minutes, add the tomatoes, thyme, oregano, and basil. Add wine and nutmeg. Raise heat and bring to a boil. Then, lower heat, stir, and simmer for 60 minutes, stirring occasionally. Add more wine if necessary and simmer for another 30 minutes on very low heat. When you're ready to serve, make the pasta according to the directions. Remove the Bolognese from the heat, add cream, and stir. Serve with spaghetti and fresh Parmesan cheese. Top with more fresh herbs, if desired.

Italian-Style Pot Roast

Serves 6

While writing an article on Yankee pot roast and its New England roots, I learned that braising meat in liquid like wine or stock goes back even further than the 1600s in early America. I've updated this humble and hearty meat dish with Italian ingredients.

3 cups reduced-sodium beef broth, divided
1 ounce dried porcini mushrooms
1 tablespoon olive oil
1 (3-pound) chuck roast
1 tablespoon pancetta or ham, chopped
1 onion, finely chopped
1 carrot, finely chopped
1 celery stalk, finely chopped
3 garlic cloves, minced

½ teaspoon salt
coarsely ground black pepper
1 bay leaf
1 tablespoon fresh sage, chopped
¼ cup fresh parsley, chopped
3 tablespoons tomato paste
3 cups dry red wine
1 (15-ounce) can whole tomatoes, drained, crushed

Heat beef broth. Add the mushrooms and soak until softened. Set aside. Heat olive oil in a large Dutch oven over medium-high heat. Add chuck roast and sear until brown on all sides, about 4 minutes per side. Transfer meat to a plate. Add pancetta, onion, carrot, and celery to the Dutch oven. Stir until golden brown. Add garlic and cook 1 minute. Season with salt and pepper. Add bay leaf, sage, parsley, tomato paste, and wine. Simmer until reduced by half, about 20 minutes. Add chuck roast, whole tomatoes, the porcini mushrooms in mushroom liquid, and 2 cups beef broth. Bring to a simmer; cover, and cook 2½ to 3 hours until meat is tender. Turn meat over halfway through cooking time. Transfer meat to a cutting board. Let stand 10 minutes before slicing. Serve with vegetables and juice.

Coffee Bourbon Brisket

Serves 6–8

Coffee and bourbon add wonderful dimensions to this already flavorful cut of meat. Prep the brisket the night before cooking so the brisket can soak in the coffee rub.

2 tablespoons finely ground coffee
2 tablespoons dark brown sugar
2 tablespoons fresh rosemary, chopped, divided
2 tablespoons thyme, chopped, divided
2 teaspoons coarse salt
2 tablespoons freshly ground black pepper
4–5 pounds beef brisket
3 tablespoons olive oil, divided
1 large white or yellow onion, sliced

1 whole bulb garlic, peeled, minced
1 cup apple cider
½ cup bourbon
1 tablespoon mustard
2 Bosc pears, sliced
½ head red cabbage, sliced
3 carrots, cut into chunks
3 potatoes, cut into chunks

The night before cooking, combine coffee, sugar, 1 tablespoon rosemary, 1 tablespoon thyme, salt, and pepper. Rub the mixture into the brisket, then wrap in plastic and refrigerate overnight. Remove brisket from the refrigerator 15 to 20 minutes before cooking. Preheat oven to 325°F. In a Dutch oven, heat 2 tablespoons olive oil over medium-high heat and brown meat, about 4 to 5 minutes per side. Remove meat from heat and add 1 tablespoon olive oil. Sauté onion until translucent, then add garlic and sauté for 1 to 2 minutes. Add cider, bourbon, and swirl in mustard. Simmer for 2 to 3 minutes. Then, add pears, cabbage, carrots, and potatoes. Place brisket on top of vegetables. Roast in the oven, covered, 1 hour per pound. Thirty minutes before cooking time is done, remove the cover. Sprinkle with remaining fresh herbs just before serving.

QUICK TIP

New York City still has a number of old-fashioned butcher shops, which I recommend frequenting for your favorite cuts of meat. My favorites are Staubitz Market, Ottomanelli's, Florence Meat Market, and Fleishers Craft Butchery.

QUICK TIP

New York City is home to what seems like a million places to buy coffee. Use whatever coffee you enjoy at home, or check out some of my favorite shops and brands: Roasting Plant, D'Amico's (I love the dark Red Hook blend), Stumptown, Blue Bottle, and Counter Culture, which I buy at Smith Canteen.

QUICK TIP

For bourbon, I've been using Four Roses Bourbon, and for mustard, I get most of my mustard from Maille. I used their tap Dijon mustard with white wine in this recipe, which I highly recommend for this and many other dishes.

WINE SUGGESTIONS

"Full-bodied Spanish reds match the powerful layers of flavor in this brisket preparation. Wines with lots of mineral depth and ample acidity such as Carignan from the Priorat or Garnacha from the Sierra de Gredos mountains near Madrid balance its richness and invigorate the palate."
—Ariana Rolich, Chambers Street Wines

Chinese Five-Spice Roasted Chicken

Serves 4–6

I recently acquired this gorgeous red chicken roaster pan, which was designed so that the heat evenly distributes through the chicken and the steam drips around the cover, making a juicier chicken. The beauty of it beckons me to make roast chicken quite often.

1 (5–6-pound) whole chicken
1 teaspoon salt
1 teaspoon freshly ground pepper
1 tablespoon Chinese five-spice
1 orange, halved

1 tablespoon Thai basil, chopped
1 tablespoon Thai basil leaves
juice of 1 orange
1 cup white wine

Preheat oven to 450°F. Clean and remove giblets from chicken. Pat dry with a towel, making sure the chicken is dry. Place the chicken in the pan. Season with salt and pepper. Rub the Chinese five-spice all over the chicken. Add the orange halves into the chicken's cavity. Sprinkle the Thai basil over the chicken and add some Thai basil leaves under the skin. Add orange juice and white wine to the bottom of the pan. Roast for 15 minutes. Lower heat to 350°F, then roast for 75 minutes.

OREGANO AND LIME ROASTED CHICKEN

Omit the Chinese five-spice and replace orange halves with lime. Top chicken with 2 tablespoons chopped fresh oregano leaves, and place 3 to 4 oregano stalks in the cavity of the chicken along with the lime halves. Add lime juice and wine to the pan. Roast according to the directions in the Chinese Five-Spice Roasted Chicken recipe.

SHAWARMA SPICE ROASTED CHICKEN

Omit the Chinese five-spice and replace orange halves with lemon. Top chicken with 2 tablespoons shawarma spice. You can buy shawarma spice mix at Kalustyan's or Patel Brothers or online from Pereg Natural Foods. Place lemon halves in the cavity of the chicken. Add juice of 1 lemon and 1 cup white wine to the bottom of the pan. Roast according to the directions in the Chinese Five-Spice Roasted Chicken recipe.

TEA-SPICED CHICKEN

Omit the Chinese five-spice and replace orange halves with lemon. Rub salt and pepper onto the chicken, to taste. Sprinkle with 2 teaspoons black tea leaves such as oolong, breakfast tea, or smoky Russian, and 1 tablespoon herbes de Provence. Add 1 cup water to the bottom of the pan, and add in 2 tea balls or tea bags full of black tea leaves. Add lemon halves to the cavity of the chicken. For this chicken, baste some of the tea to the top of the chicken every 20 minutes. Roast according to the directions in the Chinese Five-Spice Roasted Chicken recipe.

INDIAN-SPICED CHICKEN

Omit the Chinese five-spice and orange. Rub salt and pepper onto the chicken, to taste. Mix together 2 cloves minced garlic with 1 teaspoon each of cumin, coriander, and garam masala. Sprinkle over the chicken. Add wine to the bottom of the pan and roast according to the directions in the Chinese Five-Spice Roasted Chicken recipe.

Asian-Style Pot Roast

Serves 6

1 tablespoon olive oil
1 (3-pound) boneless chuck roast or beef brisket
1 cup onions, chopped
3 carrots, sliced
1 green bell pepper, chopped
6 ounces shiitake mushrooms
3 cloves garlic, minced

1 (2-inch) piece fresh ginger, minced
2 (28-ounce) cans whole tomatoes, undrained
1 cup water
2 tablespoons oyster sauce
½ teaspoon salt
1 teaspoon crushed chili pepper
1½ teaspoons Chinese five-spice powder

Add oil to a large Dutch oven over medium-high heat. Add roast or brisket and cook until brown on all sides, about 4 minutes per side. Transfer meat to a plate. Drain fat, reserving 1 tablespoon. Add onion, carrots, bell pepper, and mushrooms to Dutch oven. Cook over medium heat for 5 minutes. Add garlic and ginger. Stir until fragrant, about 1 minute. Add remaining ingredients. Bring mixture to a boil.

Add meat back in and simmer, covered, for 3 hours until meat is tender. Turn meat over halfway through cooking time. Transfer meat to a cutting board. Let stand 10 minutes before slicing. Serve with vegetables and juice.

Spiced Cornish Hens
with Harissa and Za'atar

Serves 4

Za'atar is one of my favorite savory food spices. This Middle Eastern spice mixture is usually a blend of thyme, sumac, sesame seeds, and salt. It's wonderful with poultry, but you can also sprinkle it over yogurt with a drizzle of olive oil, or as a dip with bread.

4 Cornish hens
salt and freshly ground pepper, to taste
2 tablespoons harissa
2 teaspoons za'atar
2 cloves garlic, minced

1 tablespoon fresh basil, chopped
1 tablespoon olive oil
1 large white onion, sliced
2 lemons, halved

Preheat oven to 375°F. Pat the hens dry and season with salt and pepper. Combine harissa, za'atar, garlic, basil, and olive oil. Spread over the hens. Add onion and lemon halves inside each hen. Roast in the oven for 60 to 75 minutes.

"Friends Are Coming Over" Chicken Cacciatore

Serves 4–6

Chicken cacciatore is a definite crowd pleaser, so serve this when friends are coming over. Make a side of pasta or rice to soak up the tomato sauce and be sure to serve it with some bread. Iconic Caputo Bakery bakes authentic Italian bread on the premises.

6–8 chicken pieces (thighs or breast)
⅓ cup flour
2 teaspoons salt
2 teaspoons freshly ground pepper
1 teaspoon cayenne pepper
2 tablespoons olive oil
½ cup shallots, minced
4 cloves garlic, sliced

1 green bell pepper, chopped
1 cup hearty red wine
1 (28-ounce) can crushed tomatoes
1 cup porcini mushrooms
2 tablespoons capers
1 teaspoon dried basil
1 teaspoon dried oregano
2 teaspoons fresh oregano

Pat all the chicken pieces dry. Combine the flour with salt, pepper, and cayenne. Dip each skin-side piece of chicken into the flour mixture. Add olive oil to a large sturdy skillet over medium-high heat. Place chicken skin-side down into the oil. Cook for 4 to 5 minutes on each side. Remove chicken. Add shallots and sauté until translucent. Add garlic and cook for 1 to 2 minutes. Add pepper and continue to cook. Then add wine and tomatoes. Simmer for 5 minutes. Add the mushroom, capers, and dried herbs. Simmer for 5 more minutes, adding more wine if necessary. Place the chicken back in the pan, and simmer for 30 more minutes. Top with fresh oregano.

Saturday Morning "Special Breakfast"

Smoked Salmon with All Accoutrements

Sometimes on the weekends, I create what I call a special breakfast. Like the cheese and charcuterie platter (page 30), this smoked salmon platter is full of wonderful things you can buy from produce stores and cheese shops all over NYC, such as Shelsky's of Brooklyn, or Russ & Daughters. If you want to add caviar for an extra special treat, go to a store that specializes in caviar, including Olma Caviar Boutique & Bar, Petrossian, or Royal Seafood. I hope this special breakfast inspires you to invite your friends over, steep some tea, brew some coffee, sip on a Bellini, and put the phones down to savor each other's company—that's what special breakfast is all about!

WHERE TO BUY SMOKED SALMON

Shelsky's of Brooklyn
Russ & Daughters
Pomegranate

WHERE TO BUY TEA

Prince Vladimir or Traktir from Kusmi
Brooklyn Breakfast or Chelsea Chai from The
    NYC Tea & Trading Company
Paris Ginza or Eros from Mariage Frères
Organic Assam or Brigitte's Blend from
    Harney & Sons

WHERE TO BUY COFFEE

Counter Culture
Roasting Plant
D'Amico's
Stumptown
Porto Rico Importing
McNulty's Tea & Coffee

QUICK TIP

To go along with the smoked salmon platter, I like picking up dates, figs, pomegranate seeds, pears, tomatoes, and red onions, at a fruit store like Three Guys from Brooklyn.

Sunday Morning Spicy Shakshuka

Serves 4–6

This tangy-spicy dish is very easy to make, but it's not something you'd generally eat every day of the week, so I tend to make it on Sunday mornings. Serve with some fluffy pita bread from Damascus or Kings Highway Bakery, a French baguette from Balthazar Bakery, or black olive twists from Amy's Bread. All of this, along with a strong cup of coffee, makes for a blissful breakfast.

1 tablespoon olive oil
¼ cup shallots, sliced
3 cloves garlic, minced
1 (14-ounce) can crushed tomatoes or 1 pound fresh tomatoes, chopped
1 tablespoon tomato paste
2 teaspoons harissa
2 teaspoons smoked paprika

1 teaspoon cumin
1 teaspoon salt
1½ teaspoons freshly ground pepper
½ cup goat cheese, crumbled
4–6 eggs
2 teaspoons fresh chives, chopped
2 teaspoons fresh tarragon, chopped

Preheat oven to 400°F. Add olive oil to a large skillet over medium heat. Add shallots and sauté for 1 or 2 minutes until translucent. Add garlic and cook for another minute. Add tomatoes, tomato paste, harissa, paprika and cumin. Turn down heat to low-medium and simmer for 5 to 6 minutes. Add salt and pepper. Add goat cheese, spreading it around and into the tomato mixture. Then crack desired amount of eggs right over the tomatoes. Place in oven for 8 to 10 minutes. Remove from oven and garnish with fresh herbs. You can serve this right out of the pan. My daughter puts it on ciabatta bread and makes a sandwich out of it, which I recommend.

Treats and Sweets

Who doesn't love dessert? As Julia Child so famously said, "A party without cake is really just a meeting," and I agree. I not only love to share desserts with friends and loved ones, but I love making them, and I've recently gotten my daughter on board, as well. "Let's make a pound cake," she'll say, and I never disagree. We have fun measuring and mixing, stirring and pouring, and almost always, tasting the batters and doughs of what we've concocted. Then she'll run off and play as hot cakes rise in the oven or cold desserts solidify in the refrigerator. Desserts are not only fun to eat, but they're fun to make, too, and we've turned the experience into weekend playtime.

In this chapter, you'll find some classic desserts with a twist. There's pound cake, panna cotta, a spicy chocolate cake, a clafoutis, and even a chocolate soufflé with a choice of three types of crème anglaise. In this age of gluten free and clean eating, I feel old-fashioned in my love of traditional baking. But I won't apologize. Baking is a humble, meditative act that grounds me. And shopping for ramekins, searching for cake pans, considering ingredient combinations, looking for fruit at the Asian markets to pair with spices from the Indian spice shop . . . that's my idea of fun!

Coffee Cardamom Pound Cake

Makes 1 loaf

I won't deny it that I use cardamom a lot in my recipes. Its complexity makes it one of my favorite ingredients for otherwise simple cakes and cookies. Cardamom's sweet, slightly savory, slightly herbal flavor with citrus overtones is perfect for cakes of all kinds.

1½ cups all-purpose flour
2 teaspoons baking powder
½ teaspoon salt
1 teaspoon plus 1 pinch cardamom, divided
1 cup Greek yogurt (I recommend maple yogurt)
1¼ cup sugar, divided
2 eggs

½ teaspoon vanilla
½ teaspoon coffee extract (or 1 teaspoon espresso powder dissolved in 1 teaspoon water)
¼ cup mild olive oil or vegetable oil
¼ cup plus 2 tablespoons brewed coffee
1 cup powdered sugar

Preheat oven to 350°F. Grease an 8½ x 4¼ -inch loaf pan. Combine flour, baking powder, salt, and 1 teaspoon cardamom. I use a fork or whisk to mix it until combined. In a separate bowl, combine yogurt, 1 cup sugar, eggs, vanilla, coffee extract (or espresso), and oil; whisk well. Slowly stir in flour mixture. Pour batter into prepared pan and bake for 50 to 55 minutes, until a toothpick placed in the center of loaf comes out clean. Place ¼ cup brewed coffee in a saucepan. Add remaining ¼ cup sugar. Heat until sugar dissolves. When cake is done, let cool in pan 10 minutes. Place cake on a wire rack over a sheet pan. While cake is warm, poke holes in top of cake, pour coffee mixture over top, and allow it to soak in. Let cool.

To make the icing, combine powdered sugar, remaining 2 tablespoons brewed coffee, and 1 pinch cardamom. Stir until smooth. Add more sugar if necessary to reach spreading consistency. When cake is cool, drizzle glaze over cake.

Orange Blossom Ginger Pound Cake

Makes 1 loaf

I keep a bottle of orange blossom water from Sahadi's on hand at all times. I don't end up using it as much as I'd like, but this Greek/Mediterranean/Middle Eastern water adds depth of flavor to this cake alongside the fresh ginger and orange rind. You could serve this on its own or with Frozen Banana Matcha "Ice Cream" (page 188).

1½ cups all-purpose flour
2 teaspoons baking powder
½ teaspoon salt
1 cup plain low-fat or Greek yogurt
1¼ cups sugar, divided
2 eggs

½ teaspoon vanilla extract
1 tablespoon fresh ginger, peeled, finely minced
1 tablespoon orange rind, minced
⅓ cup mild olive oil or vegetable oil
¼ cup plus 2 tablespoons fresh orange juice
1 cup powdered sugar

Preheat oven to 350°F. Grease an 8½ x 4¼-inch loaf pan. Combine flour, baking powder, and salt in a medium bowl. In a separate bowl, whisk together yogurt, 1 cup sugar, eggs, vanilla, ginger, orange rind, and oil. Slowly stir in flour mixture. Pour batter into prepared pan and bake about 50 minutes, until a toothpick placed in the center of loaf comes out clean. Place ¼ cup fresh orange juice and remaining ¼ cup sugar in a small saucepan. Heat until sugar dissolves. When cake is done, let cool in pan 10 minutes. Place cake on a wire rack over a sheet pan. While cake is warm, poke holes in top, pour orange mixture over cake, and allow it to soak in. To make glaze, combine powdered sugar and remaining 2 tablespoons orange juice, stirring until smooth and adding more powdered sugar to achieve desired consistency. When cake is cool, drizzle glaze over top of cake.

Mascarpone Semifreddo

Makes 1 loaf

Semifreddo, which means half-cold in Italian, is an elegant ice cream cake of sorts—a marriage of ice cream (but without needing an ice cream maker) and mousse, with a light and fluffy consistency. I've found them to be a fanciful (without the fuss) spring or summer dessert.

1¼ cups heavy cream
¼ teaspoon vanilla
3 egg whites, room temperature
⅓ cup sugar
½ pound mascarpone

1 tablespoon sambuca or amaretto
3 anisette cookies, crumbled, separately
¼ cup pistachios, chopped
1½ cup fresh raspberries

With an immersion blender or in a stand-alone mixer, whip the cream and vanilla together until fluffy. In a bowl, whip egg whites until frothy, but not stiff. In a separate bowl, combine sugar, mascarpone, and sambuca or amaretto. Fold in the egg whites, then fold the entire mixture into the whipped cream. Line a loaf pan with wax or parchment paper. Add ½ of the mixture into the pan, then add 2 crumbled anisette cookies and crushed pistachios. Add additional mixture, then top with remaining crumbled cookie. Top with fresh raspberries. Place in freezer for 4 or more hours. When ready to serve, cut into slices for each guest.

Chocolate Nutella Semifreddo

Makes 1 loaf

Nutella, a spread comprised of chocolate and hazelnuts, is hard to resist. Eataly has a shop devoted to this classic Italian treat.

6 ounces semisweet chocolate, chopped
(I recommend Valrhona or Jacques Torres)
¼ teaspoon sea salt
1¼ cups heavy cream
1 teaspoon vanilla
(I recommend Nielsen-Massey)

2 egg whites, room temperature
⅔ cup sugar
¼ cup Nutella, divided
2 tablespoons hazelnuts, chopped

In a double boiler, melt chocolate with salt, stirring until fully melted. Set aside and let it cool. With an immersion blender or in a stand-alone mixer, whip the cream with vanilla until fluffy (when you see soft peaks). In another bowl, whip the egg whites with sugar until you see soft peaks. Very gently fold whipped cream into the chocolate, then do the same with the egg whites until fully combined. Line a loaf pan with wax or parchment paper and pour in half of the mixture. Swirl ⅛ cup Nutella into the batter using a toothpick. Add the remaining mixture, then swirl the rest of the Nutella into the top. Sprinkle crushed hazelnuts on top. Place in freezer for 4 hours or until ready to serve.

Mango Kulfi Semifreddo

Makes 1 loaf

Kulfi is a dense Indian ice cream often served on a stick. Here, I've used some traditional ingredients found in kulfi—rosewater, saffron, cardamom, pistachios—and turned this popular Indian dessert into semifreddo.

½ cup heavy cream
6 ounces evaporated milk
6 ounces condensed milk
2 teaspoons rosewater
1 mango, puréed

1 small pinch saffron (optional)
¼ cup plus 2 tablespoons pistachios, crushed, divided
2 teaspoons cardamom
2 egg whites, room temperature

In a bowl, combine the cream and milks, stirring until blended together. Add the rosewater, mango purée, saffron, ¼ cup pistachios, and cardamom. Stir until combined. Whip egg whites until frothy. Fold into the mixture gently until combined. Line a loaf pan with wax or parchment paper. Add mixture, then top with remaining pistachios. Place in freezer for at least 4 hours or until ready to serve.

Crème Anglaise

Makes 1½ cups

Crème anglaise is a traditional French sauce that's poured over cakes, ice cream, and, in this case, into ramekins of elegant soufflés. You'll definitely want to use actual vanilla beans for this sauce to get those black flecks of fragrant vanilla.

1 cup milk
½ vanilla bean

3 large egg yolks
3 tablespoons sugar

Place a mesh strainer over a medium bowl and set aside. Pour milk into a small but heavy saucepan. Halve the vanilla bean lengthwise and, using a small spoon, scrape the vanilla seeds from the pod. Add the seeds to the milk in the saucepan and whisk until well combined. Heat the milk over medium heat, stirring often until steamy, but making sure not to let it boil. In a separate bowl, whisk the egg yolks and sugar. Gradually whisk the hot milk into the eggs until combined. Cook over low heat, stirring constantly, until the liquid turns into a custard. Be extra careful not to let the custard boil. Next, pour the custard over the mesh strainer into a bowl. Serve warm or at room temperature.

GINGER CRÈME ANGLAISE

Omit vanilla bean and add 1 (1-inch) grated piece of ginger to the milk.

ESPRESSO CRÈME ANGLAISE

You can leave in the vanilla for this, and add 1 teaspoon espresso.

Tres Leches Cake

Makes 1 (9-inch) cake

Tres leches, a well-known dessert in South America and the Caribbean, means "three milks." And indeed, this Latin American dessert does contain three different types of milk: regular, evaporated, and condensed to create a cloud-like and creamy texture.

¼ cup butter, plus extra to coat pan
1 cup flour, plus extra to coat pan
1 can evaporated milk
1 can condensed milk
¼ cup cream
1 teaspoon baking powder
¼ teaspoon salt
1 cup flour

5 eggs, yolks and whites separated
½ cup milk
1 teaspoon vanilla (I recommend Nielssen-Massey Madagascar)
1 cup sugar, divided
1 pint whipping cream
¼ cup sugar
½ teaspoon vanilla

Preheat oven to 350°F. Coat a 9 x 9-inch pan with butter and flour. Combine evaporated milk, condensed milk, and cream in a small bowl with spout. Sift together baking powder, salt, and flour. If you don't have a sifter, use a fork to mix the dry ingredients together. With a mixer, blend together ½ cup sugar with butter until fluffy. Add egg yolks and continue to beat until pale and fluffy. Add milk, then vanilla, and stir until just combined. Add this wet mixture to the dry ingredients, stirring gently until combined.

In a stand-alone mixer, beat egg whites until you see soft peaks. Pour in ½ cup sugar and continue to beat until peaks form. Add egg whites to the batter, folding it all together gently. Pour into cake pan and bake for 30 to 35 minutes. Remove from oven and let cool for 5 to 10 minutes. Remove from pan and place on a cake dish. Poke a lot of holes into the top with a fork, then pour half of the milk mixture all over the cake, so that the cake absorbs the three milks. Let sit for 15 to 20 minutes, then add remaining milk mixture. Meanwhile, whip cream with sugar and vanilla to make icing, and spread on top of cake.

Chocolate Soufflés

Makes 4 soufflés

It seems that soufflés have fallen out of fashion, but I still find them appealing. I mean, what's not to love about a warm, gooey dessert? You'll need 4 (4-inch) ramekins to make these soufflés; you can find them at the NYC Cake & Baking Distributor: a baker's paradise that sells baking tools of all sorts.

2 tablespoons plus 1 tablespoon melted butter to grease ramekins
1 cup sugar, divided
6 ounces semisweet or bitter chocolate (I recommend semisweet baking chunks from Scharffen Berger)
5 egg yolks

vanilla bean, split (or vanilla bean paste from Nielsen-Massey)
¼ cup half and half
6 egg whites
1 pinch sea salt
1 pinch cream of tartar

Preheat oven to 425°F and make sure there's enough room between the rack and roof of the oven for the soufflé to rise without touching the top. With a paper towel, spread melted butter into four ramekins. Dust with sugar and shake out the excess. Place in the refrigerator until you're ready to use them.

In a double boiler or metal bowl over a pan of simmering water, add 2 tablespoons butter with chocolate, stirring until melted and shimmering. Set aside and keep warm. (I leave it over the warm water but remove it from the burner.) In a medium-sized bowl, whisk together the yolks, vanilla, and ¼ cup of sugar. Continue to whisk until mixture is combined and thick. Slowly stir in the melted chocolate.

In a separate bowl, beat the egg whites, salt, and cream of tartar until foamy. Add the remaining sugar and continue to mix until stiff peaks are formed. Ever so gently, fold this mixture into the chocolate mixture. Combine, but don't overmix. Add the batter into the ramekins and bake for about 20 minutes or until you see the tops rise. Serve with crème anglaise, whipped cream, ice cream, or a dusting of powdered sugar.

Cardamom Cookies

Makes 12 cookies

These are my daughter's favorite cookies, so I just had to include them! These cookies are actually snickerdoodles in disguise. While snickerdoodles normally call for cinnamon, I use cardamom instead, which is one of my favorite ingredients. It has a uniquely intense aromatic scent that naturally lends itself to desserts.

QUICK TIP

I keep both cardamom pods as well as ground cardamom stocked. My most recent cardamom purchase was at Sahadi's on Atlantic Avenue in Brooklyn, but you can find cardamom at nearly any spice shop, including Kalustyan's, One for the Pot, Patel Brothers, and Spice Corner.

½ cup unsalted butter, softened
¾ cup sugar
1 egg
1¼ cups flour
¼ teaspoon salt
½ teaspoon cream of tartar
1 tablespoon cardamom
1 tablespoon sugar (I recommend Sugar In The Raw)

Blend the butter and sugar together. Add the egg and continue to beat until light and fluffy. In a separate bowl, sift and combine the flour, salt, and cream of tartar. If you don't have a sifter, simply use a fork to mix and combine. Slowly add the dry mixture into the butter mixture. Form a round ball of dough, then cover the bowl and refrigerate for at least 1 hour.

When you're ready to make the cookies, preheat oven to 400°F. Combine the cardamom and sugar in a small bowl. Roll 1 tablespoon of dough into a ball. Dip the ball into the cardamom-sugar and place on a cookie sheet. Repeat, making sure to leave enough room between the dough, as it will spread out. Bake for 10 minutes.

Vanilla Chai Pot de Crème

Serves 4–6

Making pots de crème is slightly involved, but it's definitely worth it. Out of all the desserts I make, this is one of my all-time favorites. Here, I've added in loose Chelsea Chai tea* and a whole vanilla bean. The result is sublime.

2½ cups heavy cream
½ cup milk
¼ cup sugar plus ⅓ cup sugar

1 tablespoon loose leaf chai tea or 2 tea bags
1 vanilla bean, sliced
5 egg yolks

Add the cream, milk, and ¼ cup sugar to a saucepan. Add the tea and vanilla. Bring to a simmer and stir until sugar is melted. Set aside and let steep for 30 minutes to 1 hour. Next, whip egg yolks with remaining sugar. Strain the cream mixture then slowly add it to the egg mixture, whipping continuously until combined. You can refrigerate this until you're ready to make the pots de creme. Preheat oven to 300°F and bring 6 to 8 cups of water to a boil in a teakettle. Place whatever containers you're using (ramekins or cocottes are ideal) into a pan with tall sides like a roasting pan. Add the custard into the ramekins and cover. Pour the boiling water into the pan so it comes halfway up the sides of the ramekins. Place in oven and bake for 55 minutes. Let cool, then refrigerate until ready to serve. You may also serve it warm, if you like.

COFFEE-CARDAMOM

Substitute the chai tea with 2 teaspoons ground coffee beans. Add 3 cardamom pods in place of or in addition to the vanilla and add to milk.

KAFFIR LIME

Substitute chai tea with kaffir lime leaves. In place of vanilla bean, add in kaffir or regular lime zest.

CHOCOLATE

Omit the chai tea and vanilla bean. Add 6 ounces chocolate when simmering the cream and milk.

*Chelsea Chai is an organic loose leaf tea sold on Amazon.

Coriander Cake
with Rosewater Cream and Pomegranates

Makes 1 (9-inch) cake

Adding coriander to cake might seem like a mismatch, but it's Middle Eastern in origin. I've made it bolder with rosewater cream and pomegranates.

½ cup butter, unsalted, plus extra to coat pan
1½ cup flour, plus extra to coat pan
1½ teaspoon baking powder
1 tablespoon ground coriander
¼ teaspoon salt
1 cup sugar

2 eggs
¼ cup fresh orange juice
zest of 1 orange
½ teaspoon vanilla
½ cup milk

Preheat the oven to 400°F. Butter and flour a round 8-inch cake pan. Combine flour, baking powder, coriander, and salt into a mixing bowl, using a sifter or a fork to mix well. In a separate bowl, beat together the butter and sugar. Add in eggs, one at a time. Add orange juice, orange zest, and vanilla, and mix until combined. Add the milk, and blend until the batter is all combined. Pour into the pan and bake for 30 to 35 minutes.

Make the same icing as the one used for Tres Leches Cake (page 173) but omit the vanilla and add ¼ teaspoon rosewater. Spread on cooled cake, then top with pomegranate seeds.

Earl Grey Panna Cotta

Serves 4

Panna cotta means "cooked cream" in Italian. It's often refrigerated to make a chilled dessert. Easy yet elegant, this panna cotta is made all the more enticing with Earl Grey tea. Make it the night before you want to serve so the custard can solidify.

1 cup milk
2 teaspoons gelatin powder
¼ cup sugar

½ vanilla pod and beans
1 cup cream
2 teaspoons loose leaf Earl Grey tea leaves

In a saucepan, combine milk and gelatin. Stir until combined and then turn the heat to low-medium. Stir until the gelatin is fully dissolved; be careful not to let the milk curdle or burn. Add sugar and stir until dissolved. Add vanilla beans, including pod. Remove from the heat and stir in cream and tea leaves. Let sit for 30 minutes. Strain the liquid, then pour into four ramekins. Cover and refrigerate overnight, if possible. Serve with chocolate sauce.

VANILLA BEAN PANNA COTTA

Omit the tea leaves and add in 2 teaspoons of vanilla extract in addition to the vanilla bean pod.

MATCHA PANNA COTTA

Omit the tea leaves and add in 2 teaspoons of matcha powder.

CHAI TEA PANNA COTTA

Swap out Earl Grey tea leaves for chai tea. Dust with cinnamon when serving.

Banana Bourbon Bread

Makes 1 loaf

The scent of this cake baking in the oven is intoxicating. I often make two and keep one in the freezer for when friends visit. Serve this cake as is or with ice cream, whipped cream, or icing.

⅓ cup melted butter, plus extra to grease pan
4 ripe bananas
1 egg
2 tablespoons bourbon (I recommend Four Roses Bourbon)

1 cup sugar
1½ cups flour
3 teaspoons cardamom or Cake Spice from Penzeys Spices
½ teaspoon salt

Butter a loaf pan and preheat oven to 350°F. Combine bananas, egg, and bourbon in a bowl and mash together. Add the melted butter and mash until combined. Then, add the remaining ingredients and mix until thoroughly combined. Pour batter into loaf pan. Bake for 55 minutes.

Raspberry and Blueberry Clafoutis

Makes 1 (8-inch) cake

Clafoutis is a French dessert akin to a crepe or pancake. The batter is a wonderful way to showcase summer fruits like berries and cherries. It's super easy to whip up, so be prepared to make it over and over!

2 tablespoons melted butter, plus more for buttering the pan
3 eggs
1 cup sugar
1 cup milk

1 teaspoon vanilla
½ cup flour
6 ounces blueberries
6 ounces raspberries
2 teaspoons Chambord

Preheat oven to 325°F. Butter an 8 x 8-inch baking dish. In a mixing bowl, whisk together eggs, sugar, milk, and vanilla. Add melted butter and continue to whisk. Next, add the flour and continue to whisk until smooth. Pour the batter into a cast-iron skillet or pie pan. Spread the berries around the batter. The batter may not cover the fruit, which is fine. Bake for 30 to 35 minutes or until the top is browned. Top with Chambord.

Spicy Flourless Chocolate Cake
with Rosewater Whipped Cream

Makes 1 (8-inch) cake

Spicy chocolate has become popular, so I thought I'd try it in a cake. The spiciness is balanced with the rosewater whipped cream (not shown in photo). I only add a touch of cayenne, so it won't be overly spicy. If spicy chocolate isn't appealing, simply omit the cayenne.

6 ounces bittersweet chocolate (I recommend a high-quality chocolate like Scharffen Berger or Jacques Torres)
½ cup unsalted butter
¾ cup granulated sugar
1 teaspoon vanilla
4 eggs, room temperature
¼ cup cocoa powder (I recommend a high-quality chocolate like Scharffen Berger or Jacques Torres)
⅛ teaspoon cayenne pepper
½ teaspoon cardamom (optional)
1 cup whipping cream
2 teaspoons powdered sugar, plus more for dusting
⅛ teaspoon rosewater

Preheat oven to 375°F. Butter an 8-inch round pan, free form, if possible. I use a baking pan with a removable bottom. In a double boiler over medium heat, melt chocolate with butter and stir until combined. Remove from heat and whisk in the granulated sugar and vanilla. Whisk in the eggs until combined. Add the cocoa powder, cayenne, and cardamom and continue to mix. Pour the batter into the pan and cook for 20 minutes. Remove from heat and let cool. To make rosewater whipped cream, use an immersion blender to blend whipping cream, powdered sugar, and rosewater. Dust cake with powdered sugar and serve with rosewater whipped cream or ice cream.

Rice Pudding with Lychees and Pine Nuts

Serves 4

Sweet and tart lychees, which are Chinese and Southeast Asian in origin, add a tropical flair to this classic rice pudding, while toasted pine nuts add some crunch. You can buy fresh lychees at the fruit stalls in Chinatown during the late spring when they're in season, or simply opt for canned.

1 cup rice
3 teaspoons butter, divided
1 cup milk
1 cup cream, divided
¼ cup sugar

2 tablespoons lychee liquid from the can
1 egg yolk, whipped
5–6 fresh or canned lychees, chopped
2 tablespoons pine nuts, toasted quickly in a pan over the stove

Bring 2 cups of water to a boil. Add rice and 1 teaspoon butter. Stir, cover, and let simmer for 15 to 20 minutes. When the rice is cooked, fluff the rice with a fork and add it to a medium saucepan, along with milk and ½ cup of cream. Simmer for a few minutes, then add in sugar and lychee liquid. Simmer for 15 to 20 minutes, then add in remaining cream and 2 teaspoons butter. Remove from the heat and whisk in egg yolk. Stir until combined, then fold in lychees. Top with pine nuts.

Frozen Banana Matcha "Ice Cream"

Serves 4

This recipe requires you to do a simple task ahead of time: freeze bananas overnight. It'll be worth it! This super simple recipe is as creamy as churned ice cream.

4 bananas*
1 can coconut milk
2 teaspoons matcha
½ teaspoon rosewater
1 tablespoon honey
pomegranate seeds, to garnish (optional)

QUICK TIP

You can find matcha powder at most Asian markets and also at health food shops. Be sure to buy the powder, not the tea.

Add all ingredients except pomegranate seeds to a blender. Combine until smooth. Top with pomegranate seeds or eat as is.

*The day before making this recipe, place 4 peeled bananas in a bowl and freeze them overnight.

Phyllo Tart
with Dates and Ricotta

Makes 4 tarts

It takes some adjusting to bake with phyllo dough (buttering all the layers), but once you try it, you'll be excited by how easy it is to turn these thin layers of pastry into phyllo tarts.

4 sheets phyllo dough
8 tablespoons butter
¾ cup ricotta
2 tablespoons sugar

zest of 1 orange
1 cup dates, chopped
¼ cup walnuts and/or pistachios, crushed in a
    mortar and pestle, plus more for topping

Preheat oven to 350°F. Melt butter in a small pan or in the microwave. Arrange 1 large sheet of phyllo dough on a cutting board. With a pastry brush, spread butter all over the dough. Fold in half. Spread more butter on the dough. Then fold into a triangle. Spread more butter on the dough. Repeat four more times. Combine ricotta with sugar and orange zest. Spread the ricotta onto each triangle. Top with chopped dates, walnuts, and/or pistachios. Bake in oven for about 10 minutes. Remove from oven and top with walnuts and/or pistachios.

PHYLLO TART WITH FIGS AND MASCARPONE

Swap out dates for figs, and ricotta for mascarpone.

PHYLLO TART WITH GUAVA PASTE AND PINE NUTS

Omit ricotta and dates. Mash up 2 tablespoons guava paste and mix with ¾ cup kefir cheese. Top with pine nuts.

PHYLLO TART WITH FRESH BERRIES

Mix ricotta with lemon zest instead. Top with fresh raspberries and blueberries. Drizzle berries with fresh lemon juice. Top with slivers of almonds.

NYC SHOPS AND MARKETS

Addeo Bakery
2352 Arthur Ave.
Bronx, NY 10458
718-367-8316
addeobakers.com

Adja Khady Food Distributor
251 W 116th St.
New York, NY 10026
212-933-0374

Amy's Bread
672 9th Ave.
New York, NY 10036
212-977-2670
amysbread.com

Arthur Avenue Retail Market
2321 Hughes Ave.
Bronx, NY 10458
347-590-6711
arthuravenue.com

Asia Market Corporation
71 Mulberry St.
New York, NY 10013
212-962-2020

Astor Wines & Spirits
399 Lafayette St.
New York, NY 10003
212-674-7500
astorwines.com

Balady Foods
7128 5th Ave.
Brooklyn, NY 11209
718-567-2252

Balthazar Bakery
80 Spring St.
New York, NY 10012
(212) 965-1414
balthazarbakery.com

Bangkok Center Grocery
104 Mosco St.
New York, NY 10013
212-732-8916
bangkokcentergrocery.com

Bedford Cheese Shop
265 Bedford Ave.
Brooklyn, NY 11211
and
67 Irving Place
New York, NY 10003
718-599-7588 (for both)
bedfordcheeseshop.com

Beecher's Handmade Cheese
900 Broadway
New York, NY 98101
206-956-1964
beechershandmadecheese.com

Bien Cuit
120 Smith St.
Brooklyn, NY 11201
718-852-0200
biencuit.com

Bklyn Larder
228 Flatbush Ave.
Brooklyn, NY 11217
718-783-1250
bklynlarder.com

Borgatti's Ravioli & Egg Noodles
632 E 187th St.
Bronx, NY 10458
718-367-3799

Breadberry
1689 60th St.
Brooklyn, NY 11204
718-259-6666

Brighton Bazaar
1007 Brighton Beach Ave.
Brooklyn, NY 11235
718-769-1700

Buon Italia
Chelsea Market
75 9th Ave.
New York, NY 10011
212-633-9090
buonitalia.com

Calabria Pork Store
2338 Arthur Ave.
Bronx, NY 10458
718-367-5145
calabriaporkstore.dinehere.us

Caputo Bakery
329 Court St.
Brooklyn, NY 11231
718-875-6871

Carib Food Market
1303 Fulton St.
Brooklyn, NY 11216
718-398-2324

Casa Della Mozzarella
604 E 187th St.
Bronx, NY 10458
718-364-3867

Chambers Street Wines
148 Chambers St.
New York, NY 10007
212-227-1434
chambersstwines.com

Chelsea Market
75 9th Ave.
New York, NY 10011
212-652-2110
chelseamarket.com

Damascus Bread & Pastry Shop
195 Atlantic Ave.
Brooklyn, NY 11201
718-625-7070
damascusbakery.com

D'Amico Coffee
309 Court St.
Brooklyn, NY 11231
718-875-5403
damicocoffeeroasters.com

D. Coluccio & Sons
1214 60th St.
Brooklyn, NY 11219
718-436-6700
dcoluccioandsons.com

Despaña
408 Broome St.
New York, NY 10013
212-219-5050
despanabrandfoods.com

Di Palo's Fine Food
200 Grand St.
New York, NY 10013
212-226-1033

Downtown Natural Market
1701 Church Ave.
Brooklyn, NY 11226
718-282-0110

Dual Specialty Store
91 1st Ave.
New York, NY 10003
212-979-6045
dualspecialtystorenyc.com

D'Vine Taste
150 7th Ave.
Brooklyn, NY 11215
718-369-9548

East Village Cheese
80 E 7th St.
New York, NY 10003
212-477-2601

Eataly
200 5th Ave.
New York, NY 10010
212-229-2560
and
101 Liberty St.
Brookfield Place
New York, NY 10007
eataly.com

Esposito & Sons
357 Court St.
Brooklyn, NY 11231
718-875-6863

Essex Street Market
120 Essex St.
New York, NY 10002
212-312-3603
essexstreetmarket.com

Faicco's Pork Store
6511 11th Ave.
Brooklyn, NY 11219
718-236-0119

Fei Long Supermarket
6301 8th Ave.
Brooklyn, NY 11220
718-680-0118

Fleishers Craft Butchery
192 5th Ave.
Brooklyn, NY 11217
718-398-6666
fleishers.com

Florence Meat Market
5 Jones St.
New York, NY 10014
212-242-6531

Gourmanoff
1029 Brighton Beach Ave.
Brooklyn, NY 11235
718-517-2297
gourmanoff.com

Gourmet Glatt Market
1274 39th St.
Brooklyn, NY 11218
718-437-3000
gourmetglattmarket.com

Harney & Sons Tea
433 Broome St.
New York, NY 10013
888-427-6398
harney.com

Hong Kong Supermarket
157 Hester St.
New York, NY 10013
212-966-4943

Il Buco Alimentari & Vineria
53 Great Jones St.
New York, NY 10012
212-837-2622
ilbucovineria.com

Inthira Thai Market
64-04 39th Ave.
Woodside, NY 11377
718-606-2523

Jacques Torres
Various locations
929-337-8856
mrchocolate.com

Kalustyan's
123 Lexington Ave.
New York, NY 10016
212-685-3451
kalustyans.com

Keita West African Market
1225 Broadway
Brooklyn, NY 11221

Kings Highway Bakery
292 Kings Hwy.
Brooklyn, NY 11223
718-998-0141
kingshighwaybakery.com

Kumsi Tea
1037 3rd Ave.
New York, NY 10065
347-774-2438
and
1 West 59th St.
New York, NY 10019
212-486-2843

La Bella Marketplace
7907 13th Ave.
Brooklyn, NY 11228
718-331-0050
and
99 Ellis St.
Staten Island, NY 10307
718-967-2070
labellamarkets.com

La Boîte
724 11th Ave.
New York, NY 10019
212-247-4407
laboiteny.com

La Guadalupe Fruit & Vegetables
4807 5th Ave.
Brooklyn, NY 11220
212-247-4407

Lanka Grocery
344 Victory Blvd.
Staten Island, NY 10301
718-390-0052

Le District
Brookfield Place
225 Liberty St
New York, NY 10281
212-981-8588
ledistrict.com

Maille
185 Columbus Ave.
New York, NY 10023
212-724-1014
and
927 Broadway
New York, NY 10010
929-335-6610
maille.com

Maison Kayser
Various locations
New York, NY
212-979-1600
maisonkayserusa.com

McNulty's Tea & Coffee Co.
109 Christopher St.
New York, NY 10014
212-242-5351
mcnultys.com

Mermaid's Garden
644 Vanderbilt Ave.
Brooklyn, NY 11238
718-638-1910

Millesima
1355 2nd Ave.
New York, NY 10021
212-639-9463

millesima-usa.com

Murray's Cheese
254 Bleecker St.
New York, NY 10014
212-243-3289
murrayscheese.com

Myers of Keswick
634 Hudson St.
New York, NY10014
212-691-4194
myersofkeswick.com

New Foods of India
121 Lexington Ave.
New York, NY 10016
212-679-4444
newfoodsofindia.com

New York Cake & Baking Distributor
56 W 22nd St.
New York, NY 10010
212-675-2253
nycake.com

Ninth Avenue International Foods
630 9th Ave.
New York, NY 10036
212-279-1000
ninthavenuefoodfestival.com

OLMA Caviar Boutique & Bar
1 West 59th St.
New York, NY 10019
212-371-8525
and
420 Amsterdam Ave.

New York, NY 10024
212-390-0708
olmacaviar.com

O Live
60 Broadway
Brooklyn, NY 11211
718-384-0304
olivebrooklyn.com

Oriental Pastry & Grocery
170 Atlantic Ave.
Brooklyn, NY 11201
718-875-7687

Ottomanelli Butcher Shoppe
1549 York Ave.
New York, NY 10028
212-772-7900
ottomanellibros.com

Ottomanelli & Sons Meat Market
285 Bleecker St.
New York, NY 10014
212-675-4217

Parrot Coffee
5-15 Queens Blvd.
Sunnyside, NY 11104
718-392-4515
parrotcoffee.com

Patel Brothers
37-27 74th St.
Jackson Heights, NY 11372
718-898-3445
patelbrothersusa.com

Petrossian New York Boutique
911 Seventh Ave.
New York, NY 10019
212-245-2217
petrossian.com

The Pickle Guys
49 Essex St. (btwn Grand & Hester Sts.)
New York, NY 10002
212-656-9739

Piemonte Ravioli
190 Grand St.
New York, NY 10013
212-226-0475
piemonteravioli.com

Pomegranate
1507 Coney Island Ave.
Brooklyn, NY 11230
718-951-7112
thepompeople.com

Raffetto's
144 W Houston St. (btwn MacDougal
& Sullivan Sts.)
New York, NY 10012
212-777-1261
raffettospasta.com

Roasting Plant
75 Greenwich Ave.
New York, NY 10014
and
81 Orchard St.
New York, NY 10002
212-775-7755
roastingplant.com

Royal Seafood
3100 Ocean Pkwy.
Brooklyn, NY 11235
718-996-6712

Russ & Daughters
179 E Houston St.
New York, NY 10002
212-475-4880
russanddaughters.com

Russo's Mozzarella & Pasta
363 7th Ave.
Brooklyn, NY 11215
718-369-2874
and
344 East 11th St.
New York, NY 10003
212-254-7452
russosmozzarellaandpasta.com

Sahadi's
187 Atlantic Ave.
Brooklyn, NY 11201
718-624-4550
sahadis.com

Saxelby Cheesemongers
120 Essex St.
New York, NY 10002
212-228-8204
saxelbycheese.com

Sea Breeze Fish Market
541 Ninth Ave.
New York, NY 10018
972-473-2722
seabreezefishmarkets.com

Shelsky's of Brooklyn
141 Court St.
Brooklyn, NY 11201
718-855-8817
shelskys.com

Smith & Vine
268 Smith St.
Brooklyn, NY 11231
smithandvine.com

Spice Corner
135 Lexington Ave.
New York, NY 10016
212-689-5182
sc.spicecorner29.com

Spices and Tease
Chelsea Market
and
Grand Central Terminal
New York, NY
347-470-TEAS
spicesandtease.com

Staubitz Market
222 Court St.
Brooklyn, NY 11201
718-624-0014
staubitz.com

Stinky Bklyn
215 Smith St.
Brooklyn, NY 11231
718-596-2873
stinkybklyn.com

Sullivan Street Tea & Spice Company
208 Sullivan St.
New York, NY 10012
212-387-8702
onsullivan.com

Sunrise Mart
494 Broome St.
New York, NY 10013
212-219-0033
and
12 E 41st St.
New York, NY 10017
646-380-9280

Tehuitzingo
695 10th Ave.
New York, NY 10036
212-397-5956
tehuitzingo.net

Teitel Brothers
2372 Arthur Ave.
Bronx, NY 10458
718-733-9400
teitelbros.com

The Meadow
523 Hudson St.
New York, NY 10014
212-645-4633
themeadow.com

The Meat Market
380 Tompkins Ave.
Brooklyn, NY 11216
347-528-8952
ilovemeatmarket.com

Three Guys from Brooklyn
6502 Fort Hamilton Pkwy.
Brooklyn, NY 11219
718-748-8340
3guysfrombrooklyn.com

Titan Foods
2556 31st St.
Astoria, NY 11102
718-626-7771
titanfoods.net

Tortilleria Nixtamal
104-05 47th Ave.
Queens, NY 11368
718-699-2434
tortillerianixtamal.com

Two for the Pot
200 Clinton St.
Brooklyn, NY 11201
718-855-8173

Urbani Truffles
10 West End Ave.
New York, NY 10023
212-247-8800
urbani.com

Union Square Greenmarket
E 17th St. & Union Square W.
New York, NY 10003
212-788-7476
grownyc.org

Zion Kosher Market
3802 13th Ave.
Brooklyn, NY 11218
718-436-6510

RECOMMENDED KITCHEN BRANDS AND STORES

A Cook's Companion
acookscompanion.com

All-Clad Metalcrafters
all-clad.com

Bialetti
bialetti.com

Breville
brevilleusa.com

The Brooklyn Kitchen
thebrooklynkitchen.com

Calphalon
calphalon.com

Cucina & Tavola
cucinatavola.com

Cuisinart
cuisinart.com

Duralex
duralexusa.com

Emile Henry
emilehenryusa.com

Fiestaware
fiestafactorydirect.com

Fishs Eddy
fishseddy.com

Global Table
globaltable.com

Jacques Pepin Dinnerware
surlatable.com

Jura
us.jura.com/en

KitchenAid
kitchenaid.com

Korin
korin.com

Le Creuset
lecreuset.com

Lodge
lodgemfg.com

Mauviel
mauvielusa.com

Mikasa
mikasa.com

Mrs. Meyers Clean Day
mrsmeyers.com

Nordic Ware
nordicware.com

NYC Cake & Baking Distributor
nycake.com

OXO
oxo.com

Riedel
riedel.com

Rösle
rosleusa.com

Saffron Marigold
saffronmarigold.com

Staub
staubusa.com

Sur La Table
surlatable.com

Vitamix
vitamix.com

Whisk
whisknyc.com

Williams-Sonoma
williams-sonoma.com

Wilton
wilton.com

Wüsthof
wusthof.com

ACKNOWLEDGMENTS

First, I'd like to thank my wonderful (and patient) agent Kimiko Nakamura, who called me immediately after reading my proposal to tell me much she loved it.

To Nicole Frail and Nicole Mele, my editors at Skyhorse. Thank you for taking a chance on my idea for this cookbook and for your hard work bringing it to fruition.

To Carmel D'Arienzo, Sue Ann Gleason, and the other B-School babes. I love our community and how supportive we all are to one another. Your friendship means a lot to me.

To Laurie Pzena. Thank you for all your moral support and your help cooking (and then enjoying the results).

To Karen Rossi. Thank you for your help and expertise.

To my friends, who happen to be moms, who helped me with my daughter when I was facing a deadline: Jackie Goldman, Tiphanie Gong, and Brooke Wyatt. I thank you immensely.

Thank you to Emile Henry (emilehenryusa.com) and Mauviel (mauvielusa.com), two of my favorite cookware brands, both of which offered some of their gorgeous pots, pans, and bakeware found in the book. Thank you! Your products truly make cooking a delight.

Thank you, also, to Duralex, Maille, Rosle, and Urbani Truffles. I appreciate the wonderful products and ingredients you offered.

To my family: my parents, sister, brother-in-law, three nieces, and nephew. I always love our adventures, food-related and otherwise.

To my daughter, Sabrina. Thank you for your patience as I worked on recipes, and for being daring enough to try things you'd never tasted. I'm certainly glad that the cardamom pound cake is your favorite.

CONVERSION CHARTS

METRIC AND IMPERIAL CONVERSIONS
(These conversions are rounded for convenience)

Ingredient	Cups/Tablespoons/ Teaspoons	Ounces	Grams/Milliliters
Butter	1 cup = 16 tablespoons = 2 sticks	8 ounces	230 grams
Cheese, shredded	1 cup	4 ounces	110 grams
Cream cheese	1 tablespoon	0.5 ounce	14.5 grams
Cornstarch	1 tablespoon	0.3 ounce	8 grams
Flour, all-purpose	1 cup/1 tablespoon	4.5 ounces/0.3 ounce	125 grams/8 grams
Flour, whole wheat	1 cup	4 ounces	120 grams
Fruit, dried	1 cup	4 ounces	120 grams
Fruits or veggies, chopped	1 cup	5 to 7 ounces	145 to 200 grams
Fruits or veggies, puréed	1 cup	8.5 ounces	245 grams
Honey, maple syrup, or corn syrup	1 tablespoon	.75 ounce	20 grams
Liquids: cream, milk, water, or juice	1 cup	8 fluid ounces	240 milliliters
Oats	1 cup	5.5 ounces	150 grams
Salt	1 teaspoon	0.2 ounce	6 grams
Spices: cinnamon, cloves, ginger, or nutmeg (ground)	1 teaspoon	0.2 ounce	5 milliliters
Sugar, brown, firmly packed	1 cup	7 ounces	200 grams
Sugar, white	1 cup/1 tablespoon	7 ounces/0.5 ounce	200 grams/12.5 grams
Vanilla extract	1 teaspoon	0.2 ounce	4 grams

OVEN TEMPERATURES

Fahrenheit	Celsius	Gas Mark
225°	110°	$^1/4$
250°	120°	$^1/2$
275°	140°	1
300°	150°	2
325°	160°	3
350°	180°	4
375°	190°	5
400°	200°	6
425°	220°	7
450°	230°	8

INDEX

Tracey Ceurvels